WITNESSES

BIBLE STUDY

UNIT 1 INTRO	2	**UNIT 5 INTRO**	106
1.1 Witness	4	5.1 Dignity	108
1.2 Sent	10	5.2 Compassion	114
1.3 Accountable	16	5.3 Defend	120
1.4 Grow	22	5.4 Refuge	126
UNIT 2 INTRO	28	**UNIT 6 INTRO**	132
2.1 Paradise	30	6.1 Unique	134
2.2 Captivity	36	6.2 Create	140
2.3 Rescue	42	6.3 Craft	146
2.4 Belong	48	6.4 Canvas	152
UNIT 3 INTRO	54	**UNIT 7 INTRO**	158
3.1 Pray	56	7.1 Fear	160
3.2 Share	62	7.2 Persecution	166
3.3 Kindness	68	7.3 Sacrifice	172
3.4 Patience	74	7.4 Love	178
UNIT 4 INTRO	80	**UNIT 8 INTRO**	184
4.1 Diverse	82	8.1 Awakening	186
4.2 Reach	88	8.2 Obsession	192
4.3 Context	94	8.3 Mentor	198
4.4 Understanding	100	8.4 Lead	204

Old Testament Reading Plan	210
Share Your Faith	211
Major Awards	212

 **WATCH THE VIDEO**
awanaym.org/videos

WITNESS
UNIT 01

Hey friends,

My name is Kelly Carolini. I'm a college student, lover of seafood, suspense movies, tropical beaches, and 90s video games. But above all, I love Jesus and living my life as His girl. There's nothing as sweet as actually having a close relationship with God, and it can be hard not to show it. For me, it's written on my face, and on the tip of my tongue. My heart for Jesus has a way of exposing itself, and spilling all over the place. And that's exactly how sharing the gospel can feel like in those moments, a little bit of a mess. Am I right, or am I right?

I wanted to jump all-in on a new journey, picking the brains of people who have embraced different styles and ways to answer the call in sharing their faith. I know I still have a lot to learn and I want to learn. After all, to get really good at fishing, you need to learn every knot in the book. To be honest, I've found myself in a lot of uncomfortable and frustrating situations, but I'm learning that's it's not really about me. I'm learning to look deeper into someone's frustrations or questions. Trial and error in sharing the gospel is a necessary part.

I've learned to be gracious and loving in the one-on-ones and small group chats. But even now, I still find myself tongue-tied whenever I face a big classroom well aware that I'm the only Christian present. Even harder is when I know that they know I'm a Christian. When controversial topics come up or slightly offensive jokes are made, I know others watch for my reaction. Sometimes I question myself and hesitate, not always knowing when to speak up and when to stay quiet. A part of me is still a bit afraid of the sting of public rejection, even for Jesus.

So I invite you to embark on this journey with me. And as we begin I'm asking God to grant me and you the boldness and courage to step out ... every time. To willingly go beyond our comfort zones, so God can spin it for good, and so we can become less like our yesterday-selves along the way. If we're going to do this right, we need to challenge what we think we already know about sharing the gospel. Starting with what is witnessing, and what that really means. Why does it matter? What does this look like? And how do we become one?

Your co-adventurer,

Kelly Carolini

INTRO EXPERIENCE

What is it that you can't stop talking about? Everyone has something that gets them super excited that they try to squeeze into every conversation. What is yours?

running and school

What is your thought process when that happens and why do you find yourself constantly talking about that topic?

MY PROCESS: I mention the topic because I am currently doing both of those and my friends also are.

What impact does this have on others' awareness of that topic?

It can help them on school subjects and to run more.

WATCH THE VIDEO
WITNESSES.AWANAYM.ORG

CORE CONTENT ✗ ✗ ✗ ✗ ✗ ✗ ✗ ✗ ✗ ✗

Read Matthew 5:14-16.

You are the light of the world (Matthew 5:14a, NKJV). Have you ever considered the gravity of such a statement? Think about it. Every time you walk into a dark room, you look for a light. Every time you start a car at night, the headlights come on. When the power goes out in a storm, we look for a flashlight. A light is designed with two purposes in mind—to be seen or the means by which we can see. It is designed to pierce through the darkness in order to guide, protect, and provide security.

In the famous Sermon on the Mount in the opening chapters of Matthew, Jesus reveals what it looks like to be a disciple of Christ. And it begins with light. It begins with the intention to be seen, to shed light in the darkness, and to point people in the right direction. In today's reading we see Jesus beginning His ministry explaining the mission to go into the world as a witness, to be the light of the world and to shine as a light in the darkness so that our lives can point others to God the Father.

> **WITNESS:** One who testifies regarding an event

But before Jesus gave the disciples the official word to go make disciples (Matthew 28:19), He needed to remind His first-century audience that He was there to restore Israel back to her original purpose. Now that Jesus was on the scene, the people of God's nation could finally be who they were supposed to be all along. God's original mission to Israel was to be a light (Isaiah 42:6, 49:6). She was to stand like a city on a hill—one that reflected God to all surrounding nations who looked up at her. Instead, she became just like the rest of the world. Yet now it would be Jesus who would fulfill this mission, to be the beacon of hope for the world. His crucifixion and resurrection would begin a revolution that would turn hearts and minds back to God the Father. That mission began with Jesus' disciples as witnesses of the risen Christ and the renewed mission to be the light of the world and a city on a hill. But the call to be that light extends far beyond the first disciples. Their mission was the mission of the Church. It is now our mission.

What the disciples had experienced in Jesus had fundamentally changed them and therefore compelled them to live missional lives as lights guiding, protecting, and piercing through the darkness. They lived as witnesses of the good news. Their lives became living, breathing evidence of the risen Christ. They had witnessed the entire Old Testament story reach its climax and purpose—that God's blessing would reach the whole earth.

As believers in Christ, our experience of the saving work of Christ is no less powerful and compelling and fundamentally changes who we are. We are called to be witnesses and proclaim the good news of God's blessing to the entire world. We are called to the same mission of being a light in the darkness. We, too, are called to bear witness and speak about what we have seen and heard about the risen Christ.

BASED ON THE READING, WRITE A QUESTION YOU MIGHT HAVE.

CORE CONCEPT & VERSE

CORE CONCEPT:
I am committed to speaking and living out the truth of the gospel.

READ & WRITE THIS VERSE: MATTHEW 5:16

Use the space below to help you remember this verse. Feel free to write, draw, or design in ways that make sense to you.

> In the same way, let your light shine before others, that they may see your good deeds and glorify your Father in heaven.

ABOUT THE VERSE

Matthew Chapter 5 is certainly a sermon as well as specific instructions on what a disciple of Jesus ought to look like. But Matthew 5 is also the beginning of a revolution. It is in this sermon that Jesus begins to counter much of the religious teaching of the Jewish elite. Israel had continually failed to be who God intended her to be as a light to the rest of the world. Israel reflected the world more than she reflected God. Jesus' words were not only a reminder of who Israel ought to be, but a scathing reminder of what she was not and the legalistic slavery the religious leadership had the people under.

In addition, Jesus lays the groundwork for the Church to see Jesus as the ultimate example for life, faith, and the plan God had for salvation. Jesus' words in the Sermon on the Mount serve as groundwork for the gospel message proclaimed by the apostles in the first-century church and through today.

EXPLORATION QUESTIONS

Choose two questions from below. Spend the next two days exploring them. Feel free to use reference books (like Bible dictionaries, commentaries, concordances), search online, listen to/watch sermons, and/or ask a mentor/parent/pastor. Record your findings below.

- [ ] 1. Why did Israel continue to fail in her responsibility to be salt and light to the rest of the world?
- [x] 2. Being a witness carries a big responsibility. At this moment, how prepared do you feel for the task?
- [ ] 3. Who first coined the term *city on a hill*, and what was the message being shared?
- [ ] My own question from yesterday

2. Feel prepared but it can be nerve racking
3. disobedience lack of faith and prayer

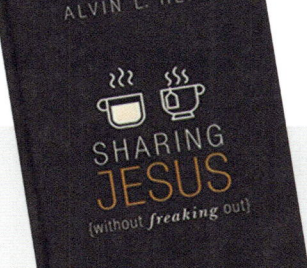

WANT TO KNOW MORE? CHECK OUT THIS BOOK!
Sharing Jesus without Freaking Out: Evangelism the Way You Were Born to Do It, by Alvin L. Reid
witnesses.awanaym.org/library

*References to websites and resources not created by Awana® are provided for your information and further study. Awana may not endorse all content of these materials.

ACTION PLAN

Based on what you have learned over the last five days about what it means to be a witness, create an action plan for yourself. What questions do you still need answered? Make a list of three to five people you could share the gospel with (family, friends, neighbors, coffee shop barista, etc.).

MY PLAN

to make a relationship with them and spread the gospel

LIST OF FIVE PEOPLE

friends
family
school mates
AC People
truck people

NOTES

in notebook

CITATION TRACK CHECKLIST >> 1.1

✓ DAYS 1-6
✓ CORE VERSES

LEADER'S INITIALS: Ea 8tr©

DATE: 11 Sept 2024

ARE YOU ON TRACK WITH YOUR BIBLE READING? RECORD WHAT YOU READ HERE:

> INTRO EXPERIENCE

Congratulations! You have been chosen as your country's youngest ever ambassador. Pick which country you would like to be an ambassador to.

COUNTRY: China

You are responsible to represent your country and to provide services and information, with clear objectives.

OBJECTIVES: to spread the gospel and to a nother job while doing it to make good relations with the people.

How do you plan to represent your country?

MY PLAN: to represent proudly but also want to spread the gospel.

> WATCH THE VIDEO
WITNESSES.AWANAYM.ORG

CORE CONTENT

Read John 20:19-23.

They were sure He was dead. They watched it happen, but now this. The tomb was empty. What would it mean for them? Would they be next? Who knew about them? What would happen now? The disciples sat in a room together, the door locked—afraid. Indeed, these questions and much more were racing through their minds. They were sure that the tomb was empty. They knew that something big had just happened, but were not at all sure what it meant.

Without warning, Jesus appears in the room. He shows them His hands and His side, almost as if He's helping them out, so they could be sure it was in fact Jesus. He brought with Him a sense of peace, assurance, and rest. There was no need to fear. There was no need to be stressed. This was *shalom*, the perfect sense of peace and wholeness. Jesus standing before them meant that everything was exactly as it should be and exactly how it was going to be in the days and years to come.

> **MISSION:** An important task or assignment with which a person has been entrusted

But Jesus also came with a mission. The disciples were told that they would be sent in the same way Jesus was sent. They would be sent with the same power, the same means, and the same mission—to make the kingdom of God a reality on this earth. The disciples would begin the Church, a missional body of believers sent to change the world, a gathering of people empowered by the Holy Spirit, to be the hands and feet of Jesus to the entire world. Jesus' impact while in human flesh was designed only to reach a limited number of people in a particular period. Jesus said that it was the Church that would do greater things (John 14:12). The Church would be sent to take the promise God fulfilled in Jesus and proclaim the good news of salvation through Christ to the ends of the earth.

We can be sent to the store for ice cream. We can be sent on a trip or vacation. We can be sent off to college. Every time we are sent—for however big or small a task—we have a mission or task to accomplish—however big or small. Being sent implies purpose and intent. Even if we are sent to wander aimlessly about the neighborhood, there is still a mission—to wander aimlessly about the neighborhood. To be sent is to be sent on a mission with a specific purpose in mind.

Just as the Father sent Jesus, so He now sends the Church. As believers in Christ, we are a part of a group sent on a Great Commission to make disciples who then go and make more disciples. This is not a suggestion or one of many options for believers in Christ, but a command. It is our mission and purpose. This is what it means to be a follower of Jesus—to walk as He did (1 John 2:6). Everything the Church is centers around making Christ known and making disciples. Jesus' intention with the disciples and also with us is to send His people into the world to bear witness to the resurrection and what it all means. The disciples would soon discover that wherever they went and whatever they would become in the years ahead, it meant they had a purpose and mission to be witnesses of the good news of the risen Christ. We have been commissioned with the same mission and purpose today.

BASED ON THE READING, WRITE A QUESTION YOU MIGHT HAVE.

CORE CONCEPT & VERSES

CORE CONCEPT:
I have been sent by God to share the gospel.

READ & WRITE THESE VERSES: MARK 16:15-16

Use the space below to help you remember these verses.
Feel free to write, draw or design in ways that make sense to you.

> Go into the whole world and proclaim the gospel to every creature. Whoever believed and is baptized will be saved, whoever does not believe will be condemned.

ABOUT THESE VERSES:

The world was turned on its ear. The man who was thought to be the Messiah, the Savior of Israel, was dead. Or was He? News had begun to travel that the tomb where Jesus was buried was empty. Some of the disciples had seen the empty tomb firsthand. Many explanations were considered. But despite their explanations, Jesus stood alive before them defying every conceivable natural law.

Fear and anxiety consumed the disciples as they gathered together trying to make some sense of this incredible event. They locked the door in fear of the Jewish authorities—in fear that what happened to Jesus might happen to them and in doubt that such a miracle was possible—even for Jesus. But in the middle of perhaps their most vulnerable moment, Jesus commissions them with the mission.

EXPLORATION QUESTIONS

Choose two questions from below. Spend the next two days exploring them. Feel free to use reference books (like Bible dictionaries, commentaries, concordances), search online, listen to/watch sermons, and/or ask a mentor/parent/pastor. Record your findings below.

- [x] 1. What did Jesus mean when He said the disciples (and the Church) would do greater things?
- [ ] 2. The disciples locked the upper room door in fear. But the disciples had the risen Jesus on their side. What could they possibly have been afraid of?
- [x] 3. If God has planted you as an ambassador in your school, town, etc., what are your objectives for proclaiming the gospel in those spaces?
- [ ] My own question from yesterday

1. that they would spread the gospel to the whole world.
3. make relationships be kind and share the gospel.

WANT TO KNOW MORE? CHECK OUT THIS BOOK!

Recovering the Full Mission of God: A Biblical Perspective on Being, Doing and Telling, by Dean Flemming
witnesses.awanaym.org/library

ACTION PLAN

Based on what you have learned over the last five days about what it means to be a witness, create an action plan for yourself. What questions do you still need answered? Make a list of three to five places you could go to share the gospel (school, neighborhood, local hangouts, etc.). Check out what Awana is doing in the country you picked in the intro activity.

MY PLAN

Try to come up with things to answer their good questions

LIST OF PLACES

school
library
xc meets
track meets
home

NOTES

CITATION TRACK CHECKLIST >> 1.2

✓ DAYS 1-6
✓ CORE VERSES

LEADER'S INITIALS: EQ Straw
DATE: 11 Sept 2024

ARE YOU ON TRACK WITH YOUR BIBLE READING? RECORD WHAT YOU READ HERE:

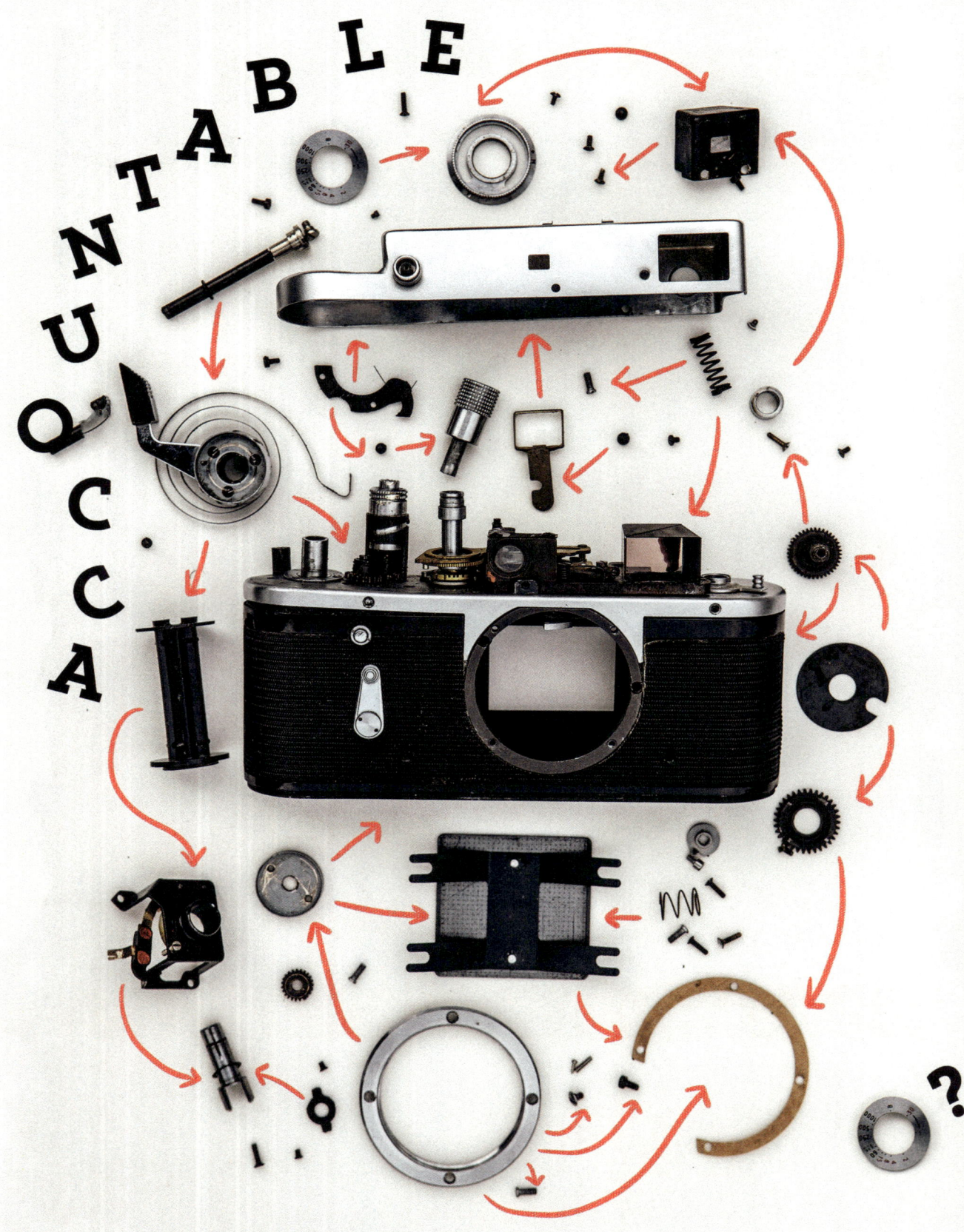

INTRO EXPERIENCE

Compare your talents with a friend's.

YOUR TALENT:	COMPARE:	A FRIEND'S TALENT:
According to you:		*According to your friend:*
TC basketball track piano cello		xc basketball track ~~piano~~ violin ~~cello~~ swim triathlon bikes
According to your friend:		*According to you:*

WATCH THE VIDEO
WITNESSES.AWANAYM.ORG

CORE CONTENT

READ ACTS 6-7.

Is it really your responsibility to share the gospel? What if it is not your gifting? What if in your lack of knowledge or skill you get something wrong? After all, didn't God give us all different gifts? Paul told the Ephesian church that some were called to be prophets, some evangelists, some teachers and pastors (Ephesians 4:11).

Remember Stephen in Acts Chapters 6 and 7? Most know his story as the guy who spoke up against the Jewish authorities and was stoned as a result. But there is something about Stephen we often forget. He was not one of the original 12 disciples. He was not a pastor of a church, nor an apostle, or even some kind of gifted evangelist. He was simply a servant of the church and a gifted leader.

We meet Stephen in Acts 6. There is a disruptive discrepancy between two different groups of Jews. The apostles understand that this need is urgent and requires attention. However, they also understand that there are those more qualified and who have more time to devote to internal matters of the church. So they do the wise thing and assign a few people to the task. This way the apostles can continue to devote their time to preaching and teaching. They chose Stephen and a few others. Stephen is described as a superstar leader (Acts 6:5-8), but while he is just doing his job, another dispute erupts and ends in Stephen being arrested. As Stephen is asked to give a testimony, he shows himself as one perfectly prepared to give an answer (1 Peter 3:15) and to be a witness. Stephen takes the Jewish authorities on a thorough theology and history lesson. He leaves nothing out. The result is Stephen's death.

Stephen understood the mission and his responsibility to proclaim the gospel when given the opportunity. It wasn't part of his official job description or part of Paul's gift list, but he knew that God had provided him everything needed when the opportunity came. Stephen was just a regular guy with an incredible passion for Jesus and the gospel.

The list Paul gives in Ephesians is not a comprehensive list of gifts nor is it relieving people of the responsibility of sharing the gospel because they are not an evangelist or pastor or teacher. For example, in the first century an evangelist was the name given to one who physically carried a message, typically one of good news. In an age without the means of mass communication, letters, messages, announcements, and news had to be carried by foot. An evangelist was a messenger who carried good news from town to town. So in the first century, the work of an evangelist was one of many means of proclaiming the gospel. Therefore, whether evangelist, teacher, pastor, or even custodian, everyone in the Church is a witness for the gospel in whatever way they've been called to serve.

> **EVANGELIST:** A person that travels from place to place proclaiming good news

So then, is it really your responsibility to share the gospel, even if it is not your exact gifting? The answer is a resounding yes! As you continue to grow in your faith and knowledge of Christ, God will continue to provide you with opportunities to be a witness. Your job is to look for the opportunities and allow God to work through you. Your job is to be faithful with the gifts you have been given and willing to step up when the time comes.

BASED ON THE READING, WRITE A QUESTION YOU MIGHT HAVE.

CORE CONCEPT & VERSES

CORE CONCEPT:
I have a unique gift and a responsibility to use it to share the gospel.

READ & WRITE THESE VERSES: EPHESIANS 4:11-16

Use the space below to help you remember these verses. Feel free to write, draw, or design in ways that make sense to you.

> So Christ himself gave the apostles, the prophets, the evangelists, the pastors and teachers, to equip his people for works of service, so that the body of Christ may be built up until we all reach unity in the faith and in the knowledge of the Son of God and become mature, attaining to the whole measure of the fullness of Christ. Then we will no longer be infants, tossed back and forth by the waves, and blown here and there by every wind of teaching and by the cunning and craftiness of people in their deceitful scheming. Instead, speaking the truth in love, we will grow to become in every respect the mature body of him who is the head, that is, Christ. From him the whole body, joined and held together by every supporting ligament, grows and builds itself up in love, as each part does its work.

ABOUT THESE VERSES:

Ephesus was a city rich in diversity. Nestled on the western edge of what is modern-day Turkey, Ephesus served as a major port city along the Aegean Sea. It was a center for diverse economic trade as well the trading of ideas and religious experience. The economic, political, and social machine of the city centered on the worship of the goddess Artemis (also known as Diana). Her temple is considered one of the Seven Wonders of the World.

Paul stayed and taught in Ephesus for nearly three years, disrupting not just their religious beliefs, but the social constructions and economy. The lucrative business of Artemis statues and books of divination came to a screeching halt. It was during this time that Paul redirected their purpose and hope.

▶ EXPLORATION QUESTIONS

Choose two questions from below. Spend the next two days exploring them. Feel free to use reference books (like Bible dictionaries, commentaries, concordances), search online, listen to/watch sermons, and/or ask a mentor/parent/pastor. Record your findings below.

☐ 1. What did Stephen say to the Jewish religious leadership that was so offensive that he deserved to be stoned?

☐ 2. How can your gifts contribute to the mission of your church?

☐ 3. Describe the process the apostles took to set up the church in Acts 6:3-7. How did they choose and delegate responsibilities of the church? Who was accountable to serve?

☐ My own question from yesterday

1. conveyed that his accusers don't respect moses or the law and the temple but necessary to worship God.
2. I can serve People and also spread the word.

WANT TO KNOW MORE? CHECK OUT THIS BOOK!
Questioning Evangelism: Engaging People's Hearts the Way Jesus Did, by Randy Newman
witnesses.awanaym.org/library

ACTION PLAN

Based on what you have learned over the last five days about what it means to be a witness, create an action plan for yourself. What questions do you still need answered? Make a list of three to five friends that have different gifts than you and brainstorm together how your unique gifts can create unity to proclaim the gospel.

MY PLAN

It is Jane's who brings the good news of God the gospel. Kate 30:9

NOTES

in notebook

CITATION TRACK CHECKLIST >> 1.3

✓ DAYS 1-6
✓ CORE VERSES

LEADER'S INITIALS: E a 8trex
DATE: 25 sept 2024

ARE YOU ON TRACK WITH YOUR BIBLE READING? RECORD WHAT YOU READ HERE:

> INTRO EXPERIENCE

Make a kite. Create your design below. Then take a look around your house and grab the materials you will need to make the kite and build it. When you are finished, see if it flies.

KITE DESIGN:

MATERIALS: String, wood, and fabric

> WATCH THE VIDEO
WITNESSES.AWANAYM.ORG

CORE CONTENT × × × × × × × × × × ×

Read Matthew 13:1-9.

If the gospel is true and Jesus is real and everything in the Bible is accurate, then why don't more people just believe? If you have ever tried to convince an atheist or skeptic about the truth of the gospel, chances are you may have felt you weren't getting through. When that happens we often start to question whether or not our efforts make any difference at all. It can be quite discouraging to feel like all the work we put into sharing the gospel can result in nothing. It is like confronting your biggest fear only to be let down in the end: a great build up of anticipation, only to be incredibly disappointed. It makes you wonder if it was worth the effort at all.

However, our efforts only take us so far. We can only be responsible for what we have control over. In this week's reading, Jesus helps His listeners see this through what they know best—farming. As a farmer, there is only so much you have control over. You can help make the ground better suited for growth, you can scatter seed at just the right time of year, and you can water that seed. But the farmer has no control over growth, only where the seed is scattered. He is responsible for doing his part. God is responsible for the outcome.

The same holds true in our responsibility to the gospel. It is not exclusively about our gifts and abilities, but rather how God uses them. In 1 Corinthians Paul comments how he may have planted the church, Apollos may have continued to pastor and lead the church, and others certainly contributed to the ministry; but their success was entirely dependent on the favor and grace of God, who made it grow (1 Corinthians 3:9). This is Jesus' parable in action in the church.

> **SOVEREIGN:**
> Possessing complete power

Some of us are outgoing and love talking to people; others are much more introverted. Some are thrilled to speak in front of large groups; others are terrified. And it seems that some people always have the right thing to say, and others would rather sit in silence. We are all wired differently but are all vital to what God is doing in this world. As we engage in the mission of God and go into the world as witnesses of the gospel, we are judged not by how many people believe as a result of our efforts or gifts, but by our faithfulness to the work God has called us to. God's mission is derived from His own great intentional and sovereign purposes. This is His mission, and the vocations, gifts, and tasks that empower us are entirely dependent on His greater purpose. He is on mission but has invited us to be coworkers with Him and for Him.

Our efforts and abilities without the Holy Spirit working through us are meaningless. God chooses to use us by using how He designed us. Being a witness is not about our abilities, success, or even our failures, but about how God creates the growth in people and the Church. We can step out into the world, live out and proclaim the gospel, fully confident that the results of our efforts are entirely up to Him. You will talk about Jesus to a lot of people in many contexts. Some will believe, many won't. But our job is to be faithful. It is about God's gospel and God's mission for God's glory.

BASED ON THE READING, WRITE A QUESTION YOU MIGHT HAVE.

- -

- -

- -

- -

CORE CONCEPT & VERSES

CORE CONCEPT:
It is God who moves people to respond to the gospel.

READ & WRITE THESE VERSES: JOHN 1:12-13

Use the space below to help you remember these verses. Feel free to write, draw, or design in ways that make sense to you.

> Yet to all who receive him to those who believed in his name he gave the right to become children of God — children born not of natural descent nor of human decision or a husband's will but born of God.

ABOUT THESE VERSES:

In the opening chapter of John's gospel we are reintroduced to the beginning, this time with Jesus as the Author of all—the incarnate Word. In Genesis we are introduced to God as the Creator and Author of all that is. We are introduced to the one who created humanity in His image. John introduces us to Jesus, God in flesh, the Creator coming as the flesh He made in His own image. In John's Gospel, we come to know God in a much more personal and intimate way.

More than just that, we also learn how we come to belong to Him. John very simply lays out the gospel message, that anyone who comes to Him is given the right to be called a child of God. In the following chapters, John explains how this is possible.

EXPLORATION QUESTIONS

Choose two questions from below. Spend the next two days exploring them. Feel free to use reference books (like Bible dictionaries, commentaries, concordances), search online, listen to/watch sermons, and/or ask a mentor/parent/pastor. Record your findings below.

- [ ] 1. Given Jesus' parable, why is discipleship such an important part of the gospel?
- [x] 2. Why do you think it is important to give God the credit when people respond to the gospel?
- [x] 3. What is your favorite example of God fulfilling His part in partnership with someone sharing the gospel?
- [ ] My own question from yesterday

Because he gave you the words and life Jesus is the one worked on the cross. The disciples they were able to commit. Where he was people and heal them.

WANT TO KNOW MORE? CHECK OUT THIS BOOK!

Creating a Missional Culture: Equipping the Church for the Sake of the World, by JR Woodward
witnesses.awanaym.org/library

ACTION PLAN

Based on what you have learned over the last five days about what it means to be a witness create an action plan for yourself. What questions do you still need answered? Pray with some of your peers, parents, or a pastor that God would use you through your gifts to help others respond to the gospel.

MY PLAN

spread the gospel at school and other places.

NOTES

in notebook

CITATION TRACK CHECKLIST >> 1.4

✓ DAYS 1-6
✓ CORE VERSES

LEADER'S INITIALS: E a Strow

DATE: 25 Sept 2024

ARE YOU ON TRACK WITH YOUR BIBLE READING? RECORD WHAT YOU READ HERE:

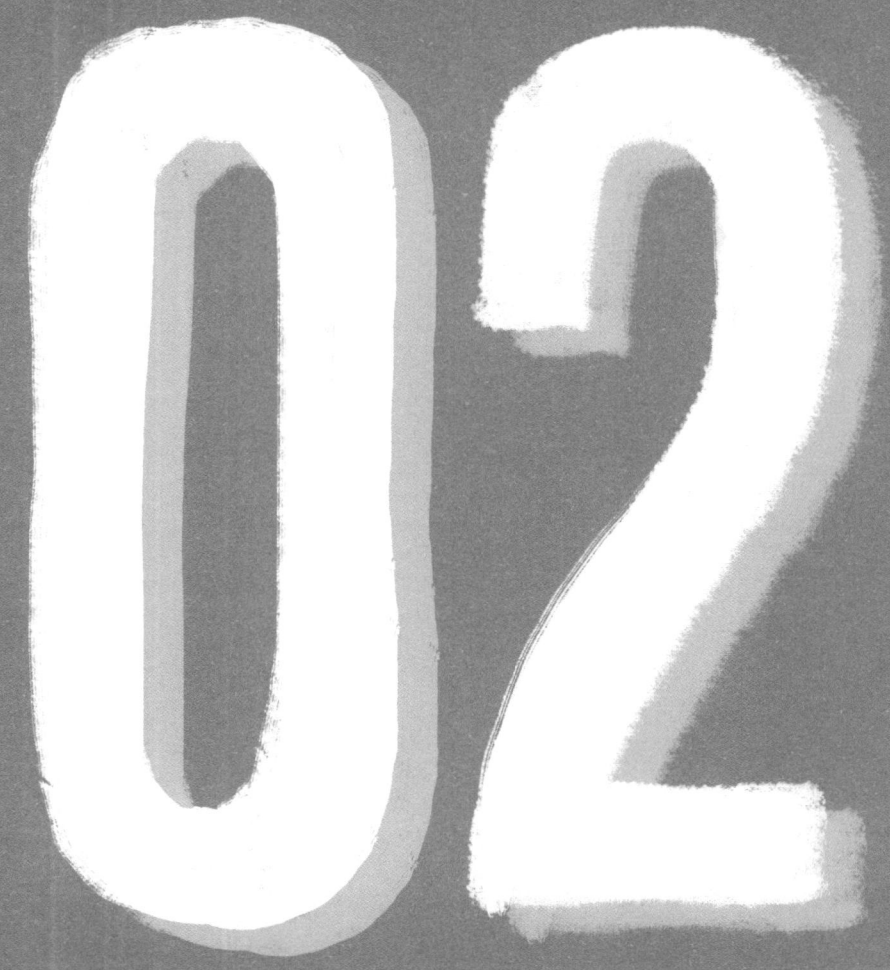

 **WATCH THE VIDEO**
awanaym.org/videos

THE GOSPEL
UNIT 02

Hey friends,

Now that we've touched base with what witnessing is, acknowledging that we are meant to use our God-given gifts and unique talents with it, and that it's very much a collaborative effort with the Holy Spirit, we can shift gears. Talking about the gospel is one thing, but what is the gospel? If someone asked me, I'd probably say that the gospel is Jesus, the living Word of God, everything Christ showed and taught us throughout His life. That's all of it, right? But when it comes to really sharing it, I'm not so sure what actually defines the gospel. I mean without the Christian lingo, how do we explain it to someone else? Or think of it ourselves? What is the gospel at its very core?

To answer these questions I flew out to Detroit and met with Harvey Carey from the Citadel of Faith Covenant Church. There he leads as pastor and advocate for his local community. Pastor Harvey showed me different parts of his city and told me stories from those areas. He was a show, not just tell, sort of guide. I found it interesting that when I asked him these very questions about what the gospel is, he answered with what it was not.

To explain what once was, and will someday be again—paradise—he challenged me to look at the remains left behind. He encouraged me to see the evidence of paradise in the brokenness. I had never looked at it from that angle before. That led us to talking about captivity and how it's all over the socioeconomic spectrum. At this point, we're so accustomed to living in captivity that we can barely recognize it anymore. It's also why it's that important to step out, and show others that there is full life outside of that. The heart of Harvey's church knows this truth very well. Many of them were rescued at different points in their lives and discovered the power and safety that came with belonging to each other as a family and ever-expanding body of Christ.

So what is that gospel message? Take this challenge with me to clearly communicate the good news. If you were writing the headline today, do you know what you would write?

Your co-adventurer,

Kelly Carolini

▶ *INTRO EXPERIENCE*

Make two perfect circles. For one of the circles draw it completely freehand. For the other use a compass or other object for assistance. How close to a perfect circle did you get when you drew the circle freehand?

CIRCLE 01:

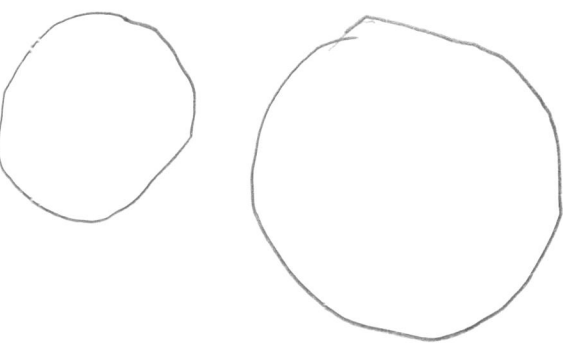

CIRCLE 02:

▶ WATCH THE VIDEO
WITNESSES.AWANAYM.ORG

CORE CONTENT

Read Genesis 1.

Paradise. Just think of it for a minute. What is paradise in your mind? Chances are it is something ideal, something perfect, and something entirely unique. Whether it is the perfect place or the perfect person, everything about it is perfect. It's paradise.

As God spoke the world into existence, He did so flawlessly—creating an absolute paradise for humanity. Everything was exactly as it needed to be, not just so that we could survive, but also so that we could thrive and have a complete relationship with Him. In the beginning, paradise was more than just being in the beautiful garden of Eden, it was being in perfect relationship with God.

When God created everything, He declared it good. In other words, He sat back and admired His work. And when it came to humanity, He created us to bear His image (Genesis 1:27, 31). So everything perfect and beautiful about God was to be reflected through us. Even though creation declares His praises and shows off His majesty and power as the Creator, it is in humanity that He wanted to show off His love, His character, His grace, and His mercy. This is actually where the gospel begins. It begins with what God desires of His creation and most of all what He desires of us. Simply being created in His image bears witness to who He is.

And yes, things went all wrong. They got downright ugly. The stain of sin masked God's beautiful creation. Our insistence to play god on our terms created something far different and far worse than what God had designed and desired for humanity. Enter Jesus—the perfect representation of the beauty of creation—the ideal of humanity. God incarnate would be humanity perfectly designed and He would instruct us to be perfect (Matthew 5:48). Be just like the Father—perfect. But how is this possible when sin has eliminated the possibility of perfection?

> **PERFECT:** Reached or completed a goal as intended

The word *perfect* in Matthew 5:48 is the Greek word *teleios*. Translated literally, the word means "complete." It carries the idea of something that has reached its goal; it is complete, finished, as intended. So when Jesus tells us to be perfect, He is taking us back to the gospel itself, back to the garden, and back to God's original intention for humanity, back to the relationship we were meant to have. The command is to be who God designed and desires you to be. It is a command to, once again, reflect the beauty of God Himself and be the perfect and beautiful reflection of the Father. But more than that, it is only because of Jesus and through Jesus that such beauty is even possible.

This is the gospel. It is the story of God's image in man, tainted and veiled by sin, but revealed in glory through Christ. It is the story of that beauty begun in paradise, if only seen in part now, on its way to be fully revealed when Christ returns and establishes the new heaven and new earth—paradise remade. The command to be perfect is a command to make God's future kingdom a present reality.

BASED ON THE READING, WRITE A QUESTION YOU MIGHT HAVE.

CORE CONCEPT & VERSE

CORE CONCEPT:
God's design for creation was goodness, beauty, and perfection.

READ & WRITE THIS VERSE: MATTHEW 5:48

Use the space below to help you remember this verse. Feel free to write, draw, or design in ways that make sense to you.

> Be Perfect, therefore, as your heavenly Father is perfect.

ABOUT THE VERSE

Some of the most famous words Jesus ever spoke are recorded in the Sermon on the Mount found in Matthew Chapters 5-7. It is likely that Matthew only provided some of the highlights, but what we get is a picture of God's ideal kingdom. The incarnation of Jesus was more than just God with us, it was the introduction of an entire kingdom. The Sermon on the Mount is the beginning of that picture being painted for us.

After correcting some serious misconceptions about what it means to be the people of God, Jesus takes His listeners back to God's intention, His goal and purpose for the part of creation formed in His image—us. In His kingdom, we are perfect.

▶ EXPLORATION QUESTIONS

Choose two questions from below. Spend the next two days exploring them. Feel free to use reference books (like Bible dictionaries, commentaries, concordances), search online, listen to/watch sermons, and/or ask a mentor/parent/pastor. Record your findings below.

1. How is Jesus' command to be perfect connected to the garden of Eden as well as the coming new heaven and new earth?

☑ 3. Look up the word *sanctification*. How does this relate to Jesus' command to be perfect?

☑ 2. Does thinking of your divine purpose in terms of perfection provide you a sense of encouragement? Why or why not?

☐ My own question from yesterday

Yes because we have a purpose. If we have a purpose we are different than other people and separate ourselves.

WANT TO KNOW MORE? CHECK OUT THIS BOOK!
Gospel: Recovering the Power that Made Christianity Revolutionary, by J.D. Greear
witnesses.awanaym.org/library

ACTION PLAN

Based on what you have learned over the last five days about what it means to be a witness, create an action plan for yourself. What questions do you still need answered? *Crafting your story*: Begin to craft your story by describing how God is continually making you perfect.

MY PLAN

Collect the word of God as news

MY STORY

by not being so perfect such as grades

NOTES

in Journal

CITATION TRACK CHECKLIST >> 2.2

✓ DAYS 1-6
✓ CORE VERSES

LEADER'S INITIALS: Ea Stroo

DATE: 25 Sept 2024

ARE YOU ON TRACK WITH YOUR BIBLE READING? RECORD WHAT YOU READ HERE:

INTRO EXPERIENCE

Fire is an incredible resource. It can save and it can destroy. Make two lists below, one list on the ways in which fire, when properly controlled, can be useful and the other list on the ways in which fire, when out of control, is dangerous.

USEFUL FIRE:	DANGEROUS FIRE:
Cooking	Brush fire
fire place	wild fire
stove	forest fire
camp fire	

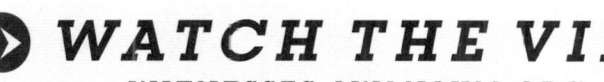

CORE CONTENT

Read Romans 1:18-32.

In the story of ancient Israel, the people's insistence to live as they chose, their desire to go their own way and ignore God's design and intention for them as God's chosen people, resulted in a weaker nation, selfish motives, and succumbing to the pressure of following the gods of the surrounding nations. As a result, Israel found herself in captivity. Israel's desire to be free from God's commands led the nation straight into slavery and bondage. Israel's story serves as a commentary for what sin has done to creation. It has tempted and lured humanity into suppressing the truth and ignoring the righteousness of God.

Paul opens his letter to the Romans with a scathing reminder of what sin has done—and more so, how God has responded. Because of sin, humanity has indeed ignored the truth, exchanged righteousness for lies, and worships creation rather than the Creator. Paul is describing a deep infection inside the human heart. It's an infection that, although we appear to be fine on the surface, runs deep into our souls. We have imprisoned ourselves and some of us don't even know it. But God, in His desire to have an authentic relationship with us, allowed us to go our own way, make our own mistakes, and even make our own gods.

Three times Paul says, God permitted them to do what they wanted (see Romans 1:24, 26, 28). God let us follow the desires of a sin-stained heart (v. 24). God allowed us to be much less than what He created us for (v. 26). God let us go our own way and do every kind of evil imaginable (v. 28). Although this kind of language seems a little harsh—almost as if God is literally giving up on us and handing us over to our own evil—that is not quite what Paul had in mind. Instead, God allows the consequences to do the teaching. He allows the sin and brokenness in our lives to hold us hostage so that we might come to desire true freedom that only God can offer through Christ. And it is in this captivity that we lose the ability to choose and live freely, and we come to know things like pain, suffering, hatred, addiction, abuse, anxiety, fear, and injustice. It is in captivity that we truly see the consequences of evil and the need for a savior.

> **CAPTIVE:** Having no freedom to choose

Israel was forced to learn much of the same lesson. For God's chosen nation, the consequences of the Israelites' actions would drive them from their land and eliminate their chances of ever seeing God's promise finally revealed. Their insistence to live on their terms would force God to hand them over to their unrighteousness so that they might know the full effect and weight of their sin.

But how much like Israel can we really be? We are not actually prisoners, right? And surely most of us are not nearly as bad as what Paul describes in his letter. We are not sitting in a cell with handcuffs or with shackles around our ankles. We are not being forced to live apart from our families in solitude. Maybe not literally, but our minds and hearts have been deceived by sin's lies. We are told that we can make the rules and that we are in control. We are reminded daily of the same lie the serpent told to Adam and Eve, that not only can we be like God, but that we can take His place. But in His great love and mercy for humanity, God did not leave us all out here to suffer as prisoners. He made a way.

Rescue is coming.

BASED ON THE READING, WRITE A QUESTION YOU MIGHT HAVE.

If I went to a point where I ignored God I wonder what would happen

CORE CONCEPT & VERSE

CORE CONCEPT:
The perfection of God's creation was corrupted when sin captured our hearts.

READ & WRITE THIS VERSE: JOHN 8:34

Use the space below to help you remember this verse. Feel free to write, draw, or design in ways that make sense to you.

Jesus replied, "very truly I tell you, everyone who sins is a slave to sin.

ABOUT THE VERSE

In an interesting exchange between Jesus and several Jews, including scribes and Pharisees, Jesus completely turns their world on its ear. Certainly used to the freedom of practicing their faith—even in the Roman-ruled world—these Jews could not seem to understand how sin could be enslaving them.

Jesus' challenge is for them to stop thinking in terms of the world and start thinking in terms of the kingdom. To the world, what might look like freedom is actually enslavement to one's own devices. True freedom is found elsewhere.

▶ EXPLORATION QUESTIONS

Choose two questions from below. Spend the next two days exploring them. Feel free to use reference books (like Bible dictionaries, commentaries, concordances), search online, listen to/watch sermons, and/or ask a mentor/parent/pastor. Record your findings below.

- [ ] 1. Why does Paul explain three times and in three different ways that God let us pursue sin?
- [ ] 2. What does it mean to practice sin, or be a slave to sin?
- [x] 3. Thinking about your life and circumstances, how would obedience to Christ create freedom instead of captivity?
- [ ] My own question from yesterday

3. Because you now lean on Him instead of yourself and forgiven by Him so have freedom but also because of not wanting to sin because you love Him.

4. Practice sin is to go to it. Slave to sin is hard it because of others and can not get out of it.

WANT TO KNOW MORE? CHECK OUT THIS BOOK!

The Screwtape Letters, by C.S. Lewis
witnesses.awanaym.org/library

ACTION PLAN

Based on what you have learned over the last five days about what it means to be a witness, create an action plan for yourself. What questions do you still need answered? ***Crafting your story:*** Think about and record what areas of your life continue to enslave you.

MY PLAN

MY STORY

NOTES

CITATION TRACK CHECKLIST >> 2.2

✓ DAYS 1-6

✓ CORE VERSES

RMP

LEADER'S INITIALS

10/15/24

DATE

ARE YOU ON TRACK WITH YOUR BIBLE READING? RECORD WHAT YOU READ HERE:

> INTRO EXPERIENCE

How much are you dependent on or attached to your phone, TV, or other electronic device?
- [ ] Pick a day this week and spend 12 hours without any electronic device.
- [ ] Be sure to communicate and coordinate with your parents beforehand.
- [ ] Every few hours record your thoughts and feelings in the spaces provided below:

TIME:	MY THOUGHTS AND FEELINGS
1:01	at school don't need it
4:01	at practice
5:01	in the car driving
6-8	hight doing my home work & don't need it

> WATCH THE VIDEO
WITNESSES.AWANAYM.ORG

CORE CONTENT × × × × × × × × × × ×

Read Luke 4:16-30.

Remember that paradise you thought of a couple of weeks ago? Imagine that no matter how hard you try you cannot get there. You can see it, imagine it, and dream of it. It is absolutely perfect. Or so you thought. That is, until Jesus. This is exactly how the nation of Israel felt. What Jesus read in today's reading was from Isaiah Chapter 61, a passage that the people of Israel read frequently about what they thought paradise would be like: a world without foreign oppression, a world without fear, a world where God ruled as king. It was a world of the promised messianic rule.

> **LIBERTY:**
> Freedom from oppression

Today's reading, although in the New Testament, takes us back to the Old Testament and the nation of Israel, which had been suffering in captivity for over 400 years—a time that God seemed to go silent. What would happen next? God created a beautiful paradise, which we ruined. God even created a plan to redeem humanity and reestablish paradise. So when was that going to happen?

Enter Jesus.

Just as people are starting to take notice of Him and news of what He is up to is starting to travel fast, Jesus enters a synagogue one Saturday and does the unthinkable. That rescue God promised was coming. Jesus says He is it. The words written down by the prophet Isaiah about the freedom from captivity, the healing of the sick, lame, and broken, and the release of the oppressed, were, in that very moment, coming true. After He reads, Jesus nonchalantly hands the scroll back to the attendant and sits back down.

Something big just happened. Jesus said He is the rescue.

The freedom we desire is found in Jesus. The rescue from sin we have been waiting for is in Jesus. The paradise we lost is found in Jesus. It was one thing for the nation of Israel to hear those words read out loud as a source of hope. Deliverance from captivity was something of a distant dream. The hope in the Messiah to come was a hope that most had, but never considered a reality. There were lots of people that rose up against oppression, claimed to be the Messiah, and ultimately failed. But none of these imposters made the claims that Jesus did. It was an entirely different thing when Jesus stood up and spoke. Isaiah was writing about more than Israel's rescue from oppressive foreign nations. He was describing a future paradise—a rescue into the kingdom of God.

Rescue is not limited to our rescue from the slavery of sin. Sure it is good to be free, but the rescue Jesus offers is more. It is redemption. It is Jesus doing what was necessary to buy humanity back and lead us to life. In other words, it is not just rescue *from* something, but rescue *to* something. The good news is the declaration of that rescue. It is a declaration that in Christ we can be brought back to paradise and back into relationship—the way God designed it to be.

Jesus reminded us that the goal is what God intended for His creation; His intention is perfection. Jesus also reminded us that although we ought to be perfect, we are slaves to sin. But the bondage of that slavery is broken when we are in Christ. Our freedom and our perfection are only found through faith in Him. We are all witnesses to what Christ has done and it is our mission to go into the world and proclaim it.

BASED ON THE READING, WRITE A QUESTION YOU MIGHT HAVE.

What would I do if I were in the situation

CORE CONCEPT & VERSES

CORE CONCEPT:
God's promise to rescue us was fulfilled in Jesus.

READ & WRITE THESE VERSES: LUKE 4:18-19

Use the space below to help you remember these verses. Feel free to write, draw, or design in ways that make sense to you.

The Spirit of the Lord is on me because he has anointed me to proclaim good news to the poor. He has sent me to proclaim freedom for the prisoners and recovery of sight for the blind, to set the oppressed free, to proclaim the year of the Lord's favor.

ABOUT THESE VERSES:

Shortly after Jesus was tempted in the desert, He began His ministry. Shortly after beginning His ministry, He returned home. Jesus no doubt knew the potential consequences that awaited Him in back in Nazareth. Yet He made a point to show up and make a significant declaration—that He was exactly what Israel had been waiting for all along. Not at all bothered by Israel rejecting Him and attempting to kill Him so early in His ministry, Jesus simply moved forward and continued to heal people, cast out demons, and proclaim the kingdom. He was the long-awaited Messiah, the Rescuer.

EXPLORATION QUESTIONS

Choose two questions from below. Spend the next two days exploring them. Feel free to use reference books (like Bible dictionaries, commentaries, concordances), search online, listen to/watch sermons, and/or ask a mentor/parent/pastor. Record your findings below.

☑ 1. What was it about Jesus' words and actions that led people from His hometown to try and throw Him off a cliff?

☑ 2. This week's verses mention some of the damage that sin brings. How does Jesus bring redemption to each of these?

☐ 3. It seemed as though many in Jesus' day were not ready for His message of rescue and redemption. What does rescue look like in your context and are you ready to hear and respond to that message?

☐ My own question from yesterday

He died on the cross for our sins.

They believed he was blasphemous by saying he is the Son of God and also believed he would save them from the Romans.

WANT TO KNOW MORE? CHECK OUT THIS BOOK!

Recovering Redemption: A Gospel Saturated Perspective on How to Change, by Matt Chandler
witnesses.awanaym.org/library

ACTION PLAN

Based on what you have learned over the last five days about what it means to be a witness, create an action plan for yourself. What questions do you still need answered? *Crafting your story*: How can (or how has) Jesus rescued you?

MY PLAN

Share the gospel

MY STORY

He rescued me from sin

> Explore how God is rescuing kids around the world through the gospel.
> **VISIT AWANA.ORG/GOGLOBAL**

NOTES

in journal

CITATION TRACK CHECKLIST >> 2.3

✓ DAYS 1-6
✓ CORE VERSES

RMP
LEADER'S INITIALS

10/15/24
DATE

ARE YOU ON TRACK WITH YOUR BIBLE READING? RECORD WHAT YOU READ HERE:

INTRO EXPERIENCE

What do you belong to? Chances are you belong to something. It could be a team or some kind of social group. This week research a well-known club or organization.

As you explore consider the following questions:

WHAT ARE THE BENEFITS OF MEMBERSHIP?

You can have access to all the gym equip. not on bring guests

WHAT IS REQUIRED TO BE A MEMBER?

to pay a monthly fee

ARE THERE ANY NEGATIVES TO MEMBERSHIP?

Yes when you want to get out of it it is hard to get out of the membership

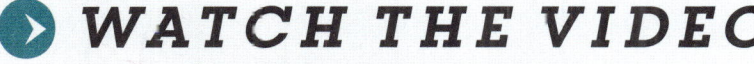

CORE CONTENT

Read John 17.

The thought of paradise can be scary. Wait, what? How could paradise create fear? Following Jesus means walking away from the world, it means living according to God's standard rather than standards of human invention. In fact, Jesus promises there will be trouble in this life (John 16:33). But Jesus never intended that we do this Christian life thing alone. If you take a look throughout the New Testament, you'll see that whenever the gospel is proclaimed, no one is ever alone. Whatever life we need to leave behind in order to follow Christ, Jesus promised a new tribe of God's people, all brought together under Christ.

> **TRIBE:** A community bonded together in Christ

In fact, this is so critical in Jesus' mind that even moments before His crucifixion this was in the forefront of His mind. While in the garden of Gethsemane, John records an amazing moment of Jesus in prayer and vulnerability. John 17 gives us a glimpse of Jesus' final moments in solitude before being arrested, put on trial, and crucified. It is in this moment that He prays for you.

This prayer, unique to John's Gospel, is sandwiched between Jesus' final instructions and His crucifixion. It provides for us a rare glimpse into Jesus' emotional state on the eve of His suffering. His humanity and divinity collide as He prays for Himself, His disciples, the mission, and every future believer.

It would be completely understandable for Jesus to be concerned with only Himself. After all, He is about to suffer the worst kind of death imaginable. Instead Jesus is concerned about His tribe. He is concerned about the unity of His disciples and the unity of every believer throughout the rest of history. In His greatest moment of angst—a moment where He, because of the huge amount of stress, sweats drops of blood—prayed that those who follow Him would do so perfectly united. And He prayed that such a supernatural display of unity would serve as a witness and show the power of the gospel.

As a follower of Christ you belong to something so much greater. As the people of God we are united in the same way that Jesus is united with the Father and the Holy Spirit. It is the kind of unity that cannot be broken. Although the Christian life promises separation from the world, it also promises to break through the barriers that often divide the world. For believers in Christ, every race, gender, social status, economic condition, nation, and culture are united as one tribe under Christ.

But there is something more than just a beautiful prayer of Christ here. Jesus' words serve as a simple and yet important reminder about our humanity. We were never designed to be alone. To be a follower of Jesus means you are in community. It means you enter into relationships that are deep and meaningful—with God and with others. You are part of a tribe. A tribe runs deeper than just a friendship or a social club. Tribes are bonded by blood—inseparable. And it is God's people who are bonded by the blood of Christ.

The paradise we long for in Christ is one shared by millions of believers all throughout history. Together, we are free from sin and called together to be the community of God's people on mission to proclaim the gospel's saving power through Christ.

BASED ON THE READING, WRITE A QUESTION YOU MIGHT HAVE.

What would a good spiritual community look like?

CORE CONCEPT & VERSE

CORE CONCEPT:
We are all invited to belong and contribute to God's tribe.

READ & WRITE THIS VERSE: 1 JOHN 3:2

Use the space below to help you remember this verse. Feel free to write, draw, or design in ways that make sense to you.

> Dear friends, now we are children of God and what we will be has not yet been made known. But we know that when Christ appears, we shall be like him, for we shall see him as he is.

ABOUT THE VERSE

In a very simple and very pastoral letter, John writes to those he has been called to shepherd about the profound simplicity of love. Despite the difficulties of following Jesus in the first century, John reminds these believers that perfect love and peace are found by abiding in Christ. He reminds them that although the world does not know or understand what it means to follow Jesus, our community, our sense of belonging, and what we consider to be home is not found in the world, but as children of God.

EXPLORATION QUESTIONS

Choose two questions from below. Spend the next two days exploring them. Feel free to use reference books (like Bible dictionaries, commentaries, concordances), search online, listen to/watch sermons, and/or ask a mentor/parent/pastor. Record your findings below.

- [x] 1. We read throughout Scripture that community is important. Why is Jesus so focused on the unity of believers moments before He is taken to His death?

- [ ] 2. What does it mean for your faith in Christ to be a part of His tribe?

- [x] 3. Where else in Scripture do you read about the benefits of belonging to God's tribe? What are they?

- [ ] My own question from yesterday

He worshiped a biblical community so we can encourage one another

Corinthians mentioned that we aren't every part of the body, is important, none is better than the other and every part is needed to thrive

WANT TO KNOW MORE? CHECK OUT THIS BOOK!

Alone Sucks: God's Cure for Our Human Crises, by Timothy Eldred
witnesses.awanaym.org/library

▶ ACTION PLAN

Based on what you have learned over the last five days about what it means to be a witness, create an action plan for yourself. What questions do you still need answered? *Crafting your story:* Who is your tribe?

MY PLAN

share gospel

MY STORY

friends family school school club

▶ NOTES

internet

CITATION TRACK CHECKLIST >> 2.4

✓ DAYS 1-6
✓ CORE VERSES

RMP
LEADER'S INITIALS

10/15/24
DATE

ARE YOU ON TRACK WITH YOUR BIBLE READING? RECORD WHAT YOU READ HERE:

 **WATCH THE VIDEO**
awanaym.org/videos

RELATE
UNIT 03

Hey friends,

On our latest endeavor, we met Pastor Harvey and several members of the Citadel of Faith Covenant Church. Their willingness to be vulnerable showed just how precious it is to belong to one another as a church family. It was such a beautiful taste of what we can expect in heaven.

I learned that what was once paradise, and will be again one day, can be known by exploring the remains and cracked pieces left behind. We've grown up with the knock-off version of God's original design. So it makes sense that we can't recognize captivity either. When it's all that you know and all that you think there is to life, unless someone shows you the alternative, it's human nature to accept it. This is also why it's so important for you and I to share with others what God has done, shown, and promised in our lives. Great! Done!

Yeah, not quite. Knowing what to say is half the challenge, the other half is how. A great place to start practicing this skill is with people close to you, such as friends and family. If that idea makes you feel a little nauseous, then welcome to the club! Let's be real, sharing our faith with loved ones, you know ... people whose opinions we actually care about, can be terrifying. But it doesn't have to be. Where are my introverted people at? I'm right there with you.

To get some guidance in how to share my faith with people, I connected with Greg Stier from Dare 2 Share ministries in Colorado. We met up on the beautiful campus of Colorado Christian University (CCU), and discussed the four major guidelines to sharing: prayer, sharing, kindness, and patience. Let's just say I had to do more than just talk the talk that day.

After all, practicing makes us better. So I challenge you to look around you. Of those you know, whom do you think you'd like to start having a conversation about God with? Bring those names to Him when you pray, and ask Jesus to lead the way. When these conversations happen, remember ask, admire, and admit if you need something to fall back on. And if you're not so sure yet, that's OK. Instead, think of whom you could start rehearsing these skills with. Maybe there's a Christian friend or classmate who would like to practice these guidelines with you. The goal is to just start practicing.

Your co-adventurer,

Kelly Carolini

▶ INTRO EXPERIENCE

Think about your conversations with God: prayer. This week pray steadfastly. Be watchful in your prayer. Be thankful in your prayer. Pray for others.

What does steadfast prayer look like in your life?

What does being watchful in prayer mean to you?

What does being thankful look or sound like in your prayer?

LIST FIVE PEOPLE

Think about the people you know or interact with on a daily basis who do not know Christ. Make a list of five people you can pray for over the course of this week.

- [ ]
- [ ]
- [ ]
- [ ]
- [ ]

▶ WATCH THE VIDEO
WITNESSES.AWANAYM.ORG

CORE CONTENT

Read Colossians 4:2-6.

When you think of prayer, what comes to mind? Church? Bedtime or dinnertime? Maybe you have said a little prayer before something difficult, like a final exam in school. For many Christians, prayer is something that they do for no reason but ritual and routine. But when you stop for a moment to pray, even if only before dinner or the big test, have you thought about the power of prayer?

Praying is far more than simply a conversation between us and Jesus. The need for Christians to pray is much like our need to breathe. It is essential to life. It is life-giving oxygen for our souls. Not only is our relationship with Christ dependent on prayer, but our ability to carry out His mission for His people is guided by prayer. God is on mission to reconcile creation with Himself in perfect unity and harmony through the cross of Christ. This mission is at the core of God's heart and it is prayer that aligns our hearts with His.

This is precisely what Paul is telling the Colossian church in today's reading. He reminds them to pray. But he does so in three specific aspects of prayer. First, he reminds them to be devoted to prayer (v. 2). Like most things you might be devoted to, devotion to prayer requires time, practice, patience, persistence, and focused dedication. Paul makes sure to remind them that prayer is not an afterthought but the core of the Christian life and mission. Second, Paul points to prayer as a means of reliance on God (v. 3). Our ability to move the gospel forward into the world is nothing of ourselves. It is all Him. Prayer has a way of taking us back to the place where we are entirely dependent on God's provision. He is the one who opens the doors and He is the one who turns people's hearts.

Finally, Paul prays for clarity. Despite our vast shortcomings, people will see and hear God through our efforts to make Him known.

Because prayer aligns us with the very heart of God, it helps us see others the way He does. Prayer helps us to care more about other people and develop deeper relationships with others. It can be through these relationships that people often best see the grace of God and the love of Christ. Prayer unites us in community and in relationship with Christ and with others. It draws us into the lives of others and creates unbreakable bonds.

> **DEVOTE:** Exclusively focus on something

Imagine walking each day in step with the will of God, prayerful that God would present you with opportunities, and to be connected to others as you pray for them. Imagine being the one God uses, through His Spirit, to be a witness to truth, preach His gospel, and introduce another to the love and saving knowledge of Christ.

Devote yourself to prayer. Be watchful and thankful for what God is doing. Pray that God would open doors and use you. Pray that you get the opportunity to proclaim *the mystery of Christ (Colossians 4:3)*. And when you do, pray that God would give you the words to be clear as you share truth in love. Finally, pray that God would open your heart to the needs of others and that you would create deeper and more impactful relationships that reflect Christ.

BASED ON THE READING, WRITE A QUESTION YOU MIGHT HAVE.

CORE CONCEPT & VERSES

CORE CONCEPT:
Prayer unites my heart with God's to see opportunities to share the gospel.

READ & WRITE THESE VERSES: COLOSSIANS 4:3-4

Use the space below to help you remember these verses. Feel free to write, draw, or design in ways that make sense to you.

ABOUT THESE VERSES:

Colossae was an ancient city nestled between Ephesus and Laodicea. This once popular commercial center had seen its height and was in decline. As was the case in many first century cities, false teachings about Christ were infecting the church. However, Colossae was somewhat unique. False teachers had infused Jewish legalism with Greek philosophy and mysticism. Paul's letter to the Colossian church confronts these errors directly.

Chapter four closes Paul's letter with a strong reminder to pray and how to treat others. Despite the many that found themselves outside the lines of the Christian faith, they were to be treated well, conversations should be full of grace, and Christians should be watchful for any opportunity that might come.

EXPLORATION QUESTIONS

Choose two questions from below. Spend the next two days exploring them. Feel free to use reference books (like Bible dictionaries, commentaries, concordances), search online, listen to/watch sermons, and/or ask a mentor/parent/pastor. Record your findings below.

☐ 1. According to Paul, why is prayer so important for the proclamation of the gospel?

☐ 2. In this week's passage, how is Paul asking the Colossians to pray in verses 2-4 and how does that set them up for what he is asking them to do in verses 5-6?

☐ 3. Think about your own prayer life. What difference do you think you can make in the lives of others simply by praying?

☐ My own question from yesterday

WANT TO KNOW MORE? CHECK OUT THIS BOOK!

Evangephobia Student Devotional: Face Your Fears and Fuel Your Passion, by Greg Stier
witnesses.awanaym.org/library

▸ ACTION PLAN

Based on what you have learned over the last five days about what it means to be a witness, create an action plan for yourself. What questions do you still need answered? Create a plan for how you are going to regularly pray for at least one person who does not know Christ.

MY PLAN

▸ NOTES

CITATION TRACK CHECKLIST >> 3.1

- DAYS 1-6
- CORE VERSES   LEADER'S INITIALS   DATE

ARE YOU ON TRACK WITH YOUR BIBLE READING? RECORD WHAT YOU READ HERE:

▶ INTRO EXPERIENCE

Think of a place or room that you visit frequently. It could be an athletic field, classroom, restaurant, etc. Take about 20 minutes and study the room carefully. Then draw the location's floor plan completely from memory. Be as detailed as possible.

ROOM:

When you are finished, revisit that location and make a list of all of the details you missed. How observant are you?

▶ WATCH THE VIDEO

WITNESSES.AWANAYM.ORG

CORE CONTENT ×××××××××××

Read Acts 16:25-31.

Think about the last time you walked past a lunch table of students you have never spoken to. What about the last time you were in line to get a coffee or the last family reunion you attended? Now be honest with yourself; during any of those times—or countless others throughout your day—did you consider it an opportune moment to stop what you were doing and share the gospel with someone? If we are honest with ourselves, most of us probably only think about being a witness when we intentionally go to the streets to share, on mission trips, or church events—not striking up a conversation with a barista about Jesus while waiting for coffee.

Yet in today's reading we see in Paul the exact kind of awareness Jesus expects of us every day as His followers—and in an unlikely place. Paul's annoyance with a demon-possessed slave girl landed him and Silas in jail after being attacked and beaten. In jail Paul and Silas spent the night praying and singing hymns. One would think, given what had just happened and their current situation, they would be trying to find a way out or lamenting over what had just transpired and praying for their freedom. Instead, Paul and Silas sang and when the moment came they were completely ready to share the gospel, even in the direst circumstances.

The earth shook, all the prison doors opened, *and everyone's bonds were unfastened* (Acts 16:26b, ESV). When most of us would take off running, Paul stuck around. Why? So he could introduce the jailer and others in the jail to Christ. Even the jailer was convinced that everyone had taken off running and was about to kill himself rather than face judgment. Paul assured him they were all there, making a clear way for the gospel.

While most of us won't be beaten or do jail time, the example set by Paul gives us a clear picture of what it means to be ready in every moment. Paul could have run once he was free and simply shared the gospel with someone else on another day. But he didn't. Instead he allowed God to use him and that circumstance to change the jailer's life forever. We could continue to walk by that lunch table every day and not say a word. We could simply get our coffee and be on our way. We could even attend every family event, create a lifetime of memories, but never utter the words of Jesus—all in hopes that a different opportunity will come to share the gospel. Yet every time you walk away without sharing Christ, you might be walking away from an opportunity that God has given you to change another's life.

> **OBSERVANT:** A watchful or keen eye

Or we could take every opportunity to allow God to use us. Jesus told His disciples to go and make disciples. Not to go when it is convenient or go when we have time—just go. Everything else ought to be secondary to the mission given to us by the Creator of the universe. God is the one who opens the doors, but we must take the first step through the doorway. So as you go about your day, hanging with friends at school, playing sports, attending family events, or just grabbing a quick coffee, think about how you interact with those around you. Look for the opportunities, pray that the Holy Spirit will help you be bold, and be ready to speak up when it's time. You never know, you might be the one God uses to change a person's life for eternity.

BASED ON THE READING, WRITE A QUESTION YOU MIGHT HAVE.

CORE CONCEPT & VERSES

CORE CONCEPT:
We must be ready in every moment to share the gospel.

READ & WRITE THESE VERSES: ROMANS 10:9-10

Use the space below to help you remember these verses. Feel free to write, draw, or design in ways that make sense to you.

ABOUT THESE VERSES:

Romans is often considered Paul's theological masterpiece. It delivers a comprehensive treatment of Christian life and faith. It is a letter that has confounded some and illuminated others to the mysteries of Christ. In it Paul uses a great deal of ink dealing with confusion of the Law given by Moses and the grace delivered via the cross of Christ. And it is in Chapter 10 that Paul confronts the Jews head-on with this reality.

Although Israel had rejected righteousness by pursuing the Law they could not keep, it made a way for the Gentiles to enter the kingdom. Any question of what is required to reunite humanity with their Creator is answered and summed up so simply—confess that Jesus is Lord.

▶ EXPLORATION QUESTIONS

Choose two questions from below. Spend the next two days exploring them. Feel free to use reference books (like Bible dictionaries, commentaries, concordances), search online, listen to/watch sermons, and/or ask a mentor/parent/pastor. Record your findings below.

☐ 1. What was the situation that landed Paul and Silas in jail and why were they worshiping while in chains?

☐ 2. What compelled Paul and Silas and all the others to stay when they could have run free?

☐ 3. Paul and Silas were ready because they were observant. How often do you see or take advantage of opportunities as they come your way?

☐ My own question from yesterday

WANT TO KNOW MORE? CHECK OUT THIS BOOK!

Gospelize Your Youth Ministry: A Spicy New Philosophy of Youth Ministry (That's 2,000 Years Old), by Greg Stier   witnesses.awanaym.org/library

▶ ACTION PLAN

Based on what you have learned over the last five days about what it means to be a witness, create an action plan for yourself. What questions do you still need answered? Take advantage of at least one opportunity to share the gospel this week. Look for it, take it, and come back and journal about it.

MY PLAN

REFLECTION:

▶ NOTES

CITATION TRACK CHECKLIST >> 3.2

- DAYS 1-6
- CORE VERSES   LEADER'S INITIALS   DATE

ARE YOU ON TRACK WITH YOUR BIBLE READING? RECORD WHAT YOU READ HERE:

 INTRO EXPERIENCE

Kindness can manifest itself in many ways. This week pick one of the choices below to be intentionally kind to someone who is either different, you don't know well, or haven't spoken to in a while.

- [ ] Visit some elderly people at a local nursing home. They often don't have many visitors and love the company.

- [ ] Now that school has begun, there are certainly plenty of new classmates that you have not met. Invite someone out for coffee after school and get to know them.

- [ ] Think of a person you have not spoken to in quite a while. Buy a card or write a personal note and send it off to them.

▶ WATCH THE VIDEO
WITNESSES.AWANAYM.ORG

CORE CONTENT

Read John 4:1-30.

One of the most hated things about Jesus was the way He treated the people the Pharisees considered terrible sinners and the lowest members of society. Jesus ate with tax collectors and sinners (Matthew 9:10), He touched people infected with leprosy (Luke 5:13), He touched and healed the unclean (Luke 8:44), and He even sat and had a conversation with a Samaritan woman. The Jewish religious leadership could not tolerate Jesus' humble approach in His interactions with those who were not like Him.

> **GRACIOUS:** Having a generous attitude and spirit

Think about your approach when you are talking about the gospel. What is more important to you, the point you are trying to make or the person you're talking to? In this week's reading, Jesus gives us the perfect example of how we ought to approach our conversations with others about spiritual matters—being entirely focused on the person and how the message of the gospel connects with their needs. It's not about just trying to close the deal.

Read John 4:1-30 a couple of times. However, instead of focusing on what Jesus says, pay close attention to how He speaks to the woman. John even makes it a point to remind us, as readers, of the enmity between Jews and Samaritans. Jews actively avoided Samaria—literally. If need be, they would go out of their way to not even step foot on their land. Yet here is Jesus hanging out with one—and a woman at that. There were vast differences between Jesus and this woman, not only culturally and socially, but even theologically. Such differences caused deep-seated division between them. But Jesus changed the game.

There are three specific ways that Jesus demonstrated how we ought to engage others in conversation about the gospel. First, despite those deep-seated differences, He saw the woman not as the world did, but as God did. More important than all the sins she had committed was her identity as a child of God. Seeing people in the proper light opens the door for a more meaningful conversation. Otherwise we risk becoming agenda driven rather than people driven. Second, Jesus connected with her in areas they could agree on. Most other Jews would have argued persuasively about where God ought to be worshiped. Instead, Jesus focused on who, not where. Finally, Jesus gently corrected her thinking without making her out to be a fool. During the course of their conversation, Jesus threw some pretty heavy concepts her way. Rightly, He was patient with her. He coached her to understanding, the kind of understanding that leads to a significant life change. And not just for her, but everyone she knew.

It is so easy for us to get caught up in trying to be right, prove our point, or get a decision for Christ that we actually spend more time insulting others rather than finding ways to connect and relate. But our actions in creating relationships with others and following Jesus' pattern with the woman at the well will communicate the gospel larger and louder than any words we use. Waxing eloquently about the saving power of Jesus and reciting verse after verse to everyone you meet will mean nothing if you treat people more like the Pharisees did and less like Jesus did.

As you continue your journey as a witness for Christ, remember that for some, their first impression of Jesus and introduction to the gospel might be you. And you never get a second chance to make a first impression.

BASED ON THE READING, WRITE A QUESTION YOU MIGHT HAVE.

_____

_____

_____

CORE CONCEPT & VERSES

CORE CONCEPT:
How we use our words matters as much as what words we use.

READ & WRITE THESE VERSES: COLOSSIANS 4:5-6

Use the space below to help you remember these verses. Feel free to write, draw, or design in ways that make sense to you.

ABOUT THESE VERSES:

Once again we are back in Colossae, and Paul is dealing with the false teachers that had infused Jewish legalism with Greek philosophy and mysticism. Paul's continued final instructions go beyond just speaking up or fighting against those luring people away from truth. It is not just what one says, but how it is said.

A person's speech should be *gracious* and *seasoned with salt* (ESV). In other words pleasant, attractive, and winsome. Answering another in wisdom requires speaking to outsiders in a way that communicates the teachings of Christ as well as the manner of Christ.

EXPLORATION QUESTIONS

Choose two questions from below. Spend the next two days exploring them. Feel free to use reference books (like Bible dictionaries, commentaries, concordances), search online, listen to/watch sermons, and/or ask a mentor/parent/pastor. Record your findings below.

1. Under normal circumstances with any other Jew, how would this woman have been treated and what does Jesus do differently?

2. What are three ways Jesus demonstrated kindness to the woman at the well?

3. Despite the potential gossip and scandal, Jesus still treated the woman with compassion and respect. How can you demonstrate the same kindness Jesus showed to someone who is different than you? Give a specific example.

My own question from yesterday

WANT TO KNOW MORE? CHECK OUT THIS BOOK!

Dare 2 Share: A Field Guide to Sharing Your Faith (Focus on the Family), by Greg Stier   witnesses.awanaym.org/library

ACTION PLAN

Based on what you have learned over the last five days about what it means to be a witness, create an action plan for yourself. What questions do you still need answered? Make a plan this week to act intentionally to treat someone in the same way Jesus would.

MY PLAN

NOTES

CITATION TRACK CHECKLIST >> 3.3

☐ DAYS 1-6
☐ CORE VERSES   LEADER'S INITIALS   DATE

ARE YOU ON TRACK WITH YOUR BIBLE READING? RECORD WHAT YOU READ HERE

▶ INTRO EXPERIENCE

Every year around the holiday season there are reports of people waking up before the sun rises to start shopping and even people who sometimes spend days waiting in line for the latest and greatest products. What are you willing to wait for?

LIST THE TOP FIVE THINGS FOR WHICH YOU WOULD BE WILLING TO WAIT IN LINE FOR MORE THAN FIVE HOURS.

1.
2.
3.
4.
5.

▶ **WATCH THE VIDEO**
WITNESSES.AWANAYM.ORG

CORE CONTENT ××××××××××

Read 2 Timothy 2:14-26.

We live in a world of instant gratification. The faster the better. We travel faster, a package can arrive across the world in a matter of days, information is instant, and communication is constant. It seems that in every way we have a greater capacity to have more and we have it faster than ever. Except when it comes to patience. Our ability to gain instant access to almost anything has made us some of the most impatient people in the world. Generally speaking, Western culture demands more and it demands faster, but with less work and less commitment. Can such a mentality work when it comes to being a witness?

In Paul's second letter to Timothy, he is near the end of his life and preparing Timothy to take a more prominent position of leadership in the church. Paul is passing the baton to Timothy to continue to carry out the mission. Timothy has patiently waited and learned from Paul and this final letter is Paul's highlights and final reminders. Timothy is reminded that this gospel thing is going to have its problems. Some people will be all in; others, however, will stray away (vv. 20-21). He is reminded not to get entangled with the things that distract him from the task at hand (vv. 22-23). Finally, Paul reminds Timothy to be patient. Be patient with those who will not listen and those who will purposefully cause trouble and controversies—patience for the sake of the gospel. To put it simply, Timothy must communicate and emulate such a high degree of patience that an opponent is compelled to listen and thus embrace the truth.

> **LONGSUFFERING:**
> Patience despite trouble

According to Paul, patience on Timothy's part will help create an atmosphere of forgiveness and open the door for repentance. In other words, Timothy's patience allows him to gently correct others so that *God may perhaps grant them repentance leading to a knowledge of the truth* (v. 25, ESV). Just as we noted last week with Jesus and the woman at the well, Jesus' ability to build a relationship—even if only briefly—hinged entirely on Him being patient with her. His patience helped lead her to correction and repentance. Patience creates a space for the gospel to be heard.

You may not be leading a church—yet. But while Timothy was dealing with false teachers and direct threats to the proper teachings of the church, Paul's encouragement to be patient still applies as you continue on this journey of becoming an effective witness of the risen Christ. Over the course of your life you will engage in all kinds of conversations. Some of them will require you to spend a significant amount of time building relationships over many years. You will quickly discover that one conversation is not enough. You may need supernatural amounts of patience as you slowly and carefully lead someone down a path that takes him or her to Christ. Still other conversations may be a one-shot opportunity. However, the same patience is required. You may feel the pressure of trying to close the deal. Yet while trying to be faithful you end up further hardening a person's heart.

As you meet others, build relationships, and seek ways to introduce others to Jesus, remember that your preparedness also means using words that are gracious, that you are others-focused, and that you have an attitude of patience as you engage in conversation.

BASED ON THE READING, WRITE A QUESTION YOU MIGHT HAVE.

CORE CONCEPT & VERSE

CORE CONCEPT:
Leading others to faith and trust in Christ requires persistence and patience.

READ & WRITE THIS VERSE: PROVERBS 25:15

Use the space below to help you remember this verse.
Feel free to write, draw, or design in ways that make sense to you.

ABOUT THE VERSE

Solomon was considered the wisest of all kings These proverbs, collected by the men of King Hezekiah, provide practical wisdom for everyday life and speak to the interest of the king as he rules and administers government matters within God's kingdom. These particular proverbs are meant to give insight to the king. While a king cannot know the mysteries of God's kingdom rule, his job is to rule as God's representative in human affairs.

> EXPLORATION QUESTIONS

Choose two questions from below. Spend the next two days exploring them. Feel free to use reference books (like Bible dictionaries, commentaries, concordances), search online, listen to/watch sermons, and/or ask a mentor/parent/pastor. Record your findings below.

☐ 1. In light of the challenges Timothy was facing, how would being patient with others make a difference and represent better leadership for the church?

☐ 2. How many other verses about patience can you find? Write out at least three and share what you learned from this search.

☐ 3. In our fast-paced—right now—Western culture, how would patience benefit you and your ability to witness to others?

☐ My own question from yesterday

WANT TO KNOW MORE? CHECK OUT THIS BOOK!

Reach Out, Don't Freak Out Student Devotional, by Greg Stier
witnesses.awanaym.org/library

ACTION PLAN

Based on what you have learned over the last five days about what it means to be a witness, create an action plan for yourself. What questions do you still need answered? Practice patience. Make a plan on how you will invest your time and effort into another person so that they might come to know Jesus.

MY PLAN

NOTES

CITATION TRACK CHECKLIST >> 3.4

- DAYS 1-6
- CORE VERSES   LEADER'S INITIALS   DATE

ARE YOU ON TRACK WITH YOUR BIBLE READING? RECORD WHAT YOU READ HERE:

 **WATCH THE VIDEO**
awanaym.org/videos

CONTEXT
UNIT 04

Hey friends,

On our last trip, we began to sink our feet into the water by practicing Greg Stier's methods for sharing. Whether you've started with a solid Christian friend or stepped out to have a faith conversation with someone who isn't a believer, I'm so proud. If I've learned anything from our last challenge, it is that the tension between how far to push and how deep to listen doesn't necessarily go away. As it's said in Colossians 4:6 *Let your conversation be always full of grace, seasoned with salt, so that you may know how to answer everyone* (NIV). And this, my friends, means that though practice will make us better, it should never not keep us on our toes. Sharing is complex, but the core remains the same. We must always be kind and patient when we speak about Jesus. But also, and I myself sometimes forget, we need to be just as faithful, to the sharing of the gospel. So step out, and let the Holy Spirit step in.

And it's not just the sharing part that you have to learn. People, too, are complex. Different people come from different contexts, different walks of life, and require different approaches that are meaningful to them. This is as true now as it's been for centuries. But what does it really look like historically? How can we learn people? To dig deeper, I reached out to Ed Stetzer at Wheaton College, where we revisited C.S. Lewis' work and his intentionality in presenting the gospel in a way that was mindful of the needs of the people of his time. Then, walking through the Billy Graham Center, we visited the efforts and triumphs of Christ-followers who lived their lives as great witnesses.

All of this reminded me that the gospel is not bound by a few continents or groups of people, but that it goes beyond oceans and mountains, capturing the hearts of vastly different people with the same truth. Stetzer helped me to understand that the gospel is quite the world traveler. It embraces cultural diversity and enters into any context, transforming the lives of everyone it encounters. I knew this in my mind, but had never stepped aside to understand it.

So now I pass the torch to you, and challenge you to write notes of the different cultures and contexts that are present around you. Jot down the cultures of friends, classmates, and co-workers. Think about the contexts that people around you have grown up in.

Realize that your story, your knowledge and understanding of the gospel, is one narrative. Everyone has his or her own narrative. Think about how your own background, context, and upbringing impacted your understanding of the gospel, and what that means as you influence another person's narrative.

Your co-adventurer,

Kelly Carolini

▶ INTRO EXPERIENCE

There have been many horrendous events in history that were a direct result of excluding groups of people (e.g., the Holocaust, the Rwandan genocide, slavery). Research an event and answer these questions below.

MY RESEARCH:

What was the event you researched?

Who made up the group of oppressors?

Who made up the excluded group of people and what were they excluded from?

Describe the event.

How did the excluded group suffer?

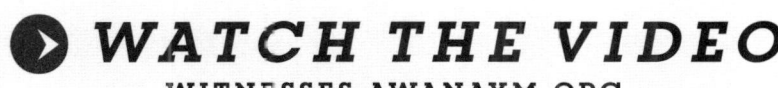

▶ WATCH THE VIDEO
WITNESSES.AWANAYM.ORG

CORE CONTENT ✕ ✕ ✕ ✕ ✕ ✕ ✕ ✕ ✕ ✕ ✕

Read Acts 10:9-43.

When you think of church, what comes to mind? The building? The hour-long service on Sunday mornings? What about the people? At its core, God's intention for the Church has always revolved around the gathering of His people, and more importantly the diversity of that gathering. Yet for many of us we find ourselves going to church with people who live in our neighborhoods, who look like us, speak like us, and worship like us. We are drawn to those who share the same interests and life experiences. But when something different enters our familiar space, it feels out of place and uncomfortable.

From the very beginning the nation of Israel was called to be God's chosen people, a people intended to be different, holy, and set apart in such a way that people might see God in them. But Israel's status as chosen was not for their own benefit alone, but for the sake of the rest—for the sake of the Gentiles.
God's story of one nation was so that all nations could taste salvation.

This is precisely the reason for Peter's vision in this week's reading. Up to this point in Acts, the gospel was largely preached to the Jews. But now, Peter is asked to come to the house of a centurion named Cornelius after Cornelius is given a vision to send for Peter. At that same moment Peter is also given a vision. The vision is filled with animals Jews considered to be unclean and should not eat. However, he is given the command to rise, kill, and eat (v. 13). Of course—being the good Jew that he is—Peter refuses. But what Peter learns quickly is that this vision is much less about food and more about the gospel itself. Three times this vision happens until he is interrupted by the invitation to come and visit Cornelius.

> **COMMUNITY:** A group of people who come together with shared values, experiences, or beliefs

The Church was always designed to be diverse. All of God's people gathered in the name of Christ. Israel once thought Gentiles were not only forbidden from entering the main center of the Temple to participate in worship, but they were considered unclean. Just being in the presence of Gentiles made Jews unclean. They went to great lengths in order to avoid defilement. But this vision is precisely what Paul describes in his letter to the Ephesian church. The dividing wall is no longer standing, there is no longer any reason for hostility, and the Gentiles are no longer strangers and aliens to the gospel. The Gentiles are now heirs together with Israel, joined together as one Body who now both share in the promise in Christ (Ephesians 3:6).

There is beauty in diversity. To be diverse literally means to be different. But the Church is also a community. It is a unity of everyone together. This is the Church brought together by the gospel and placed under Christ, every nation, tribe, and language beautifully diverse and perfectly united. The gospel was never intended to be restricted to one people, but given to *one* people with the purpose of taking it to *every* people. So as you seek to take the gospel and speak truth, seek out those that Christ would seek first. Seek those who seem not to fit in the spaces the world has cut out, because then the gospel will fit perfectly.

BASED ON THE READING, WRITE A QUESTION YOU MIGHT HAVE.

CORE CONCEPT & VERSES

CORE CONCEPT:
There is no culture or ethnicity excluded from the gospel message.

READ & WRITE THESE VERSES: EPHESIANS 2:14-16

Use the space below to help you remember these verses. Feel free to write, draw, or design in ways that make sense to you.

ABOUT THESE VERSES:

Paul's letter to the Ephesians was written to a Gentile community who needed a reminder regarding their place in the kingdom. Gentiles were allowed to believe and worship, but from a distance, separated from the Jews. This, of course, created tension and hostility between the two groups. But the death and resurrection of Jesus changed all of that.

According to Paul, to be in Christ meant that there was unity in diversity. No longer would the Jews be the exclusive heirs of the kingdom. The Gentiles now had a place at the table and rights in the family of Abraham and would be declared adopted sons and daughters of God.

EXPLORATION QUESTIONS

Choose two questions from below. Spend the next two days exploring them. Feel free to use reference books (like Bible dictionaries, commentaries, concordances), search online, listen to/watch sermons, and/or ask a mentor/parent/pastor. Record your findings below.

1. How did Peter's response in this passage differ from Cornelius' response to God in Acts 10:3-6?

2. How was Peter's obedience to God to reach out and share the gospel with the Gentiles who were sent to him in contradiction to the customs and traditions of Israel?

3. Being very honest and transparent, is there any partiality that you, your family, or your friends show toward the lost? Explain. How will you address this?

My own question from yesterday

WANT TO KNOW MORE? CHECK OUT THIS BOOK!

Compelled: Living the Mission of God, by Ed Stetzer and Philip Nation
witnesses.awanaym.org/library

▶ ACTION PLAN

Based on what you have learned over the last five days about what it means to be a witness, create an action plan for yourself. What questions do you still need answered? How will you embrace people from all cultures and ethnicity and build a community to reflect the diversity Jesus called for in His Church?

MY PLAN

▶ NOTES

CITATION TRACK CHECKLIST >> 4.1

DAYS 1-6

CORE VERSES   LEADER'S INITIALS   DATE

ARE YOU ON TRACK WITH YOUR BIBLE READING? RECORD WHAT YOU READ HERE:

▶ INTRO EXPERIENCE

Draw as many logos, brands, or items you can think of that are recognized in almost every country, language, and culture (e.g., Coca-cola).®

▶ **WATCH THE VIDEO**
WITNESSES.AWANAYM.ORG

CORE CONTENT

Read Acts 15:1-19.

Last week we learned that actions Jesus took to reconcile His people to God were always intended for all people and that Israel was simply the vehicle by which God chose to deliver the message. But while the promises of God may be for all, is the gospel message suitable for all cultures and contexts? Or are we, at times, trying to fit a square peg into a round hole? Does the message have to change in order to connect people with Christ?

This was precisely the question that Paul and Barnabas had to take on in the early church. It was not long after Peter had his experience with Cornelius and the Holy Spirit came to the Gentiles, confirming that Gentiles are descendants of Abraham as well. Paul and Barnabas were assigned the task of sorting through what Gentile inclusion now meant in the context of the Church. In other words, should the Gentiles participate in the religious customs of the Jews and the law of Moses, or had something changed?

Now that Peter had experienced the Holy Spirit being poured out on the Gentiles, it was clear that salvation comes through belief rather than ritual. It was the Spirit who would cleanse the heart of the Gentiles by faith (v. 9). Paul and Barnabas confirm Peter's comments and they conclude that any unnecessary barriers to belief or participation in the Church ought to be removed and the essentials for belief clarified.

Known as the Jerusalem Council, this gathering of early Christian leaders did several things for this young movement. It solidified the unity between Jews and Gentiles, it gave confirmation that Gentiles were part of the promise given to Abraham, and it showed us the coming worldwide impact the gospel would have as it made waves beyond the Jewish world. But more than that, the Jerusalem Council made it clear that the promise of salvation would be relevant in every context and culture. Because the gospel would be grounded in belief, the location would not matter, the people group would not matter, nor would the circumstances matter. The message of salvation by grace through Christ would serve as the unbreakable thread tying together every people of every nation.

> **GENTILE:** The designation of anyone not Jewish

It seems easy—almost natural—for us to either force people into the way we worship or conversely change the message because we are trying to be relevant. However, either side of that spectrum is missing the mark. The mission of being a witness is proclaiming the core of the gospel message as it has always been. It transcends time, space, and cultures. Our goal is to become like Peter and Paul—masters of understanding their audience and finding ways to speak truth in a way that does not compromise the message but connects to the hearts of people.

Chances are you won't have to leave your city or town to experience different cultures and contexts. Whether at school, work, or even with family, you encounter diversity. Stick to the truth. Stick to the gospel. It is never our job to make the gospel appealing or relevant. It is only our job to find ways to connect our audience to a message that is life-changing.

BASED ON THE READING, WRITE A QUESTION YOU MIGHT HAVE.

CORE CONCEPT & VERSE

CORE CONCEPT:
The promise of salvation is relevant in every culture and context.

READ & WRITE THIS VERSE: GALATIANS 3:28

Use the space below to help you remember this verse.
Feel free to write, draw, or design in ways that make sense to you.

ABOUT THE VERSE

Acts is in large part a history book detailing three specific transitions: A geographic transition from Jerusalem to the rest of the world, a theological transition from a Jewish understanding of the gospel to a universal understanding, as well as a cultural shift from Jew to Gentile. The Jerusalem Council in Acts Chapter 15 is the culmination of all of these transitions.

It is here that we witness Peter, Paul, Barnabas, and many other key leaders in the early church come together to sort through precisely what it means to believe in Jesus, what constitutes salvation, and what is required of those—from all cultures—who call themselves Christians.

▶ EXPLORATION QUESTIONS

Choose two questions from below. Spend the next two days exploring them. Feel free to use reference books (like Bible dictionaries, commentaries, concordances), search online, listen to/watch sermons, and/or ask a mentor/parent/pastor. Record your findings below.

☐ 1. How are the expectations of how God wants us to change similar or different than what the Jewish Christians expected from the Gentiles when they believed?

☐ 2. How does the gospel transcend culture or context?

☐ 3. How do the gospel and the Church unite cultures and contexts?

☐ My own question from yesterday

WANT TO KNOW MORE? CHECK OUT THIS BOOK!

Subversive Kingdom: Living as Agents of Gospel Transformation, by Ed Stetzer
witnesses.awanaym.org/library

▶ ACTION PLAN

Based on what you have learned over the last five days about what it means to be a witness, create an action plan for yourself. What questions do you still need answered? What do you need to stop doing and start doing in order to stick to the gospel message in every context?

MY PLAN

Find out how Awana looks in other countries.
VISIT AWANA.ORG/GOGLOBAL

▶ NOTES

CITATION TRACK CHECKLIST >> 4.2

- DAYS 1-6
- CORE VERSES   LEADER'S INITIALS   DATE

ARE YOU ON TRACK WITH YOUR BIBLE READING? RECORD WHAT YOU READ HERE:

 INTRO EXPERIENCE

Write a list of conversation starters you can use with someone you've never met before.

- [ ]
- [ ]
- [ ]
- [ ]
- [ ]
- [ ]

This week, talk to at least two people you've never met using your conversation starters. Make the conversation last more than five minutes if you can.

Was it easy or difficult to maintain a conversation more than five minutes? Why?

_____

_____

_____

_____

_____

_____

_____

CORE CONTENT

Read 1 Corinthians 9:19-23.

Have you ever tried to maintain a long conversation with someone with whom you have nothing in common? You do everything you can to stay engaged and interested in the conversation, but none of the things they talk about are of any interest to you. Maybe it was last night's football game and you know nothing about football. Or perhaps they are discussing the latest political commentaries—something you lost interest in months ago. Although God's intention for humanity is to be perfectly united in Christ, we maintain a wide variety of contexts and, therefore, an even wider diversity, making it all the more difficult to find the desire to share the gospel whenever we are presented with the opportunity.

> **CONTEXT:** The interrelated setting, environment, language, and conditions in which something or someone exists

Yet once again, it is Paul who provides us with just the right example for how to carry out the mission not only in contexts we are comfortable with, but in all contexts. In fact, Paul gives us a strategy for how we ought to intentionally pursue new and different contexts. In this week's passage the Corinthian church, confused on several levels and having sought advice from Paul on several different questions, seems to also question his apostolic authority. In Paul's humility and desire to boast only in Christ, he asks nothing of the church and therefore renounces any stake in a particular person or ideology.

Paul's goal is to connect with everyone so that they might gain Christ. And for Paul that meant becoming all things to all people. But what in the world did Paul mean? It sure sounds like he is willing to sin in order to reach sinners, or to become something he is not in order to reach people different than him. However, this is not at all what Paul is getting at. This is Paul's humility and genuine love for others on display.

It would have been easy for Paul to consider himself somehow superior to others because of his knowledge, his status, and even his encounter with Jesus. Instead, he essentially puts himself in the shoes of the Corinthians. He wants to understand them, reach them, and be certain they know Christ fully. Paul does not elevate himself over others or demand anything from others. He remains a servant of others and displays a high degree of empathy for those he is ministering to.

It is so much easier to elevate ourselves over others and find every reason to ignore our mission to be a witness. This week's challenge is to follow the example of Paul as he follows the example of Christ. The challenge is to be empathetic towards others. Be humble. And the next time you find yourself stuck in a conversation with a person with whom you have nothing in common, take the time to learn about them and embrace the differences. But don't just wait for new contexts to come knocking at your door. Seek them out. Get beyond your comfort zone and seek out ways that you can be all things to all people so that through you, God may save some.

BASED ON THE READING, WRITE A QUESTION YOU MIGHT HAVE.

- -

- -

- -

- -

CORE CONCEPT & VERSES

CORE CONCEPT:
Sharing the gospel requires seeking out new contexts and befriending people who need Christ.

READ & WRITE THESE VERSES: 1 CORINTHIANS 9:22-23

Use the space below to help you remember these verses. Feel free to write, draw, or design in ways that make sense to you.

ABOUT THESE VERSES:

The first-century Corinthian church was littered with problems. They displayed a lack of humility, a misunderstanding of the resurrection, and some significant sexual sins—all of which prevented them from being a unified, growing body of Christ. And although they sought answers from Paul, they even questioned Paul's authority to answer those very questions.

Paul patiently yet firmly addresses each concern they raise as well as several of his own concerns. But at every turn his point remains the same—love Christ, love each other, and be united. These young Corinthian believers needed to see that the gospel message and the unity of the church had nothing to do with them or Paul, or anyone else. But it has everything to do with Christ.

▶ EXPLORATION QUESTIONS

Choose two questions from below. Spend the next two days exploring them. Feel free to use reference books (like Bible dictionaries, commentaries, concordances), search online, listen to/watch sermons, and/or ask a mentor/parent/pastor. Record your findings below.

☐ 1. Describe the context in which Paul was writing in this passage.

☐ 2. How do you respond to questions or differing conclusions to faith issues?

☐ 3. How can you follow Paul's example to be all things to all people and still maintain your identity and commitment to Christ?

☐ My own question from yesterday

WANT TO KNOW MORE? CHECK OUT THIS BOOK!

Breaking the Missional Code: Your Church Can Become a Missionary in Your Community, by Ed Stetzer and David Putman   witnesses.awanaym.org/library

▶ ACTION PLAN

Based on what you have learned over the last five days about what it means to be a witness, create an action plan for yourself. What questions do you still need answered? List two people outside your church that you will befriend.

MY PLAN

MY STORY

▶ NOTES

CITATION TRACK CHECKLIST >> 4.3

- DAYS 1-6
- CORE VERSES   LEADER'S INITIALS   DATE

ARE YOU ON TRACK WITH YOUR BIBLE READING? RECORD WHAT YOU READ HERE:

LESSON 4.3 CONTEXT // DAY 5

Understanding

INTRO EXPERIENCE

Become a student of your own culture. Research your local town or the closest city and learn all about it. Or, if you have been on or are planning on doing a mission trip, you could choose to study the country you visited or will be going to.

Location:

Population:

Brief history of the town/city/country:

Ethnic makeup:

Languages spoken:

Life expectancy:

Religious makeup:

Government structure:

What kind of work do people do?

Are there any agricultural or industrial exports?

How do you think the culture you described could impact someone's faith experience?

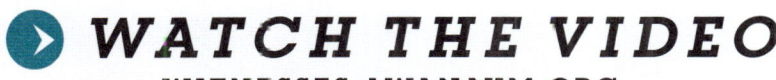

CORE CONTENT

Read 1 Chronicles 12:23-37.

Consider this scenario: You get on board an airplane at your local airport to an unknown destination. Your plane lands and you make your way through the jetway. As the narrow tunnel opens, lights and sounds emerge as if you are entering an entirely new world. You look around to gather your bearings only to realize that none of the signs are in your native language. You have no knowledge of where you are, how to get out, and no one to ask. What is the first thing you do?

> **WISDOM:** Accumulated experience and knowledge used with good judgment

In order to get to the exit, you would need to gather information and understanding of your location, the language, and the general layout of the airport. Before any progress is made, you need significant understanding. It wouldn't matter how confident you were, or how fast you could run through the airport. The same is true when being a witness.

Now consider the nation of Israel: Israel wanted a king. They got Saul. But in order to flourish as the nation God had intended, they would need something better. They would need David. This week's reading provides the details of David's conquering of Jerusalem and the establishment of his kingdom. Chronicles catalogs the men who joined David's stronghold. Among these people were 200 leaders from the tribe of Issachar. While most of the other tribes listed were noted as warriors, Issachar was different and the writer of Chronicles made certain we noticed.

This long list of supporters for David's inauguration as king illustrates the incredible enthusiasm the people had for David. Saul had failed, God's will for David was clear, and the people were on board. But despite the strong backing of military might, strength, tenacity, and loyalty, without a degree of wisdom the effort would have been severely impaired. Enter the people of Issachar. Along with military might, you need intelligence. You need people who understand the situation, the times, the culture, etc. Without wisdom and understanding, enthusiasm and confidence can only take you so far.

As people on mission for Christ, we, of course, must have enthusiasm, confidence, and strength. But we must also have wisdom and understanding. We must be students of the world around us so that we can read the signs and find our way. That means we have to get beyond our own comfort zone and learn about people unlike us, learn about cultures and contexts different than ours, and yet embrace these people as children created by an almighty God. It is not enough to simply know the gospel and how to talk about Jesus. It is not enough to exude confidence and boldness when preaching the gospel to anyone who will listen. It is not enough be willing to walk up to a stranger and strike up a conversation and turn it into a spiritual awakening. All of those are great and necessary. But we must continually seek to learn more about the people around the world and in our own backyard. We need to be able to step off the jetway into any context and be ready to share the good news of Jesus Christ.

BASED ON THE READING, WRITE A QUESTION YOU MIGHT HAVE.

CORE CONCEPT & VERSE

CORE CONCEPT:
I must continually learn and understand more about the cultures and contexts surrounding me.

READ & WRITE THIS VERSE: PROVERBS 4:7

Use the space below to help you remember this verse.
Feel free to write, draw, or design in ways that make sense to you.

ABOUT THE VERSE

When reading through Proverbs, it becomes very clear, very quickly that the key to understanding—whether each other, our culture, or even God—stems from having wisdom and understanding its value in our lives. Chapter 4 of Proverbs is broken into a couple of different parts. This first section—running through verse 9—paints for us a picture of what it looks like to pass wisdom down from one generation to the next.

Specifically, verse 7 focuses in on the motivation for wisdom and the willingness to chase after it and do whatever it takes to gain understanding. Knowledge and understanding will not come by passively waiting, they are gained by active seeking.

EXPLORATION QUESTIONS

Choose two questions from below. Spend the next two days exploring them. Feel free to use reference books (like Bible dictionaries, commentaries, concordances), search online, listen to/watch sermons, and/or ask a mentor/parent/pastor. Record your findings below.

- [ ] 1. Who in Scripture demonstrates being a good student of culture? Why and how do they demonstrate it?
- [ ] 2. What other verses teach us how to develop wisdom?
- [ ] 3. Whom do you know that is wise and practices great wisdom? Describe him or her.
- [ ] My own question from yesterday

WANT TO KNOW MORE? CHECK OUT THIS BOOK!

Compelled by Love: The Most Excellent Way to Missional Living, by Ed Stetzer and Philip Nation
witnesses.awanaym.org/library

ACTION PLAN

Based on what you have learned over the last five days about what it means to be a witness, create an action plan for yourself. What questions do you still need answered? In what area of your life do you need more wisdom? Whom will you talk to this week to help you practice good judgment in this area?

MY PLAN

NOTES

CITATION TRACK CHECKLIST >> 4.4

	DAYS 1-6		
	CORE VERSES	LEADER'S INITIALS	DATE

ARE YOU ON TRACK WITH YOUR BIBLE READING? RECORD WHAT YOU READ HERE:

 **WATCH THE VIDEO**
awanaym.org/videos

JUSTICE
UNIT 05

Hey friends,

We are officially halfway into our journey! Insane. On the last trip, our conversation with Ed Stetzer emphasized the importance of considering context as we strive to understand where people are coming from. For years now, I've known that whenever we stop to listen to other people, we get glimpses of their ongoing joys and challenges. These glimpses are a great way to gently peek into someone's heart and get a sense of their pain, often filling us with compassion in return. So what then? What do we do after we know how much someone is hurting? How do we, as God's children, put compassion into action?

Because these questions are ambitious, so must be our search to answer them. We begin with a trip to the beautiful African country of Uganda. It is a place that has drawn out the hearts of many organizations and ministries, including Awana®, Compassion International®, and the Navigators™. But it has also tugged at the hearts of individuals who saw a need, and devoted their God-given abilities to meeting it. To help us process and bring all that was learned home, I flew out to Colorado Springs. Because who can better give insights on walking out compassion than the former president and CEO of Compassion International himself Wess Stafford. The conversation with both Wess and the experts in Uganda addressed the need to respond to the dignity of others in order to be stirred with compassion, giving us the opportunity to step up and advocate for others, while ultimately connecting them to our only real refuge—Jesus Christ.

As you make your way through, I challenge you to look for patterns in what is said and shown. I was amazed by how much stayed the same, even when situations were different. Make note of these. Outside of the material, I challenge you to look at the people you pass by and encounter throughout your day as humans, created in His image. Not at their clothes or car or phone. Look at their eyes. Peek into their hearts. And see how the Lord moves you to genuinely share your faith once you truly care for them first as a person.

Your co-adventurer,

Kelly Carolini

DIGNITY

leader smart artistic ave thoughtful

> INTRO EXPERIENCE

Make a list of words that communicate a person's dignity (e.g., loved, respected).

Make a list of words that are used to strip people of their dignity (e.g., worthless, loser).

How often do you hear or use words from either list when describing people?

_____
_____
_____
_____
_____
_____

> WATCH THE VIDEO
WITNESSES.AWANAYM.ORG

> CORE CONTENT

Read Zechariah 7, Matthew 23:1-12, 23-24.

There is a special condition of the human nature that grants every person who has ever existed value and worth far beyond anything they could ever earn. Dignity in today's culture is often seen as something to be earned or a standard of behavior. You may have heard statements like he acts in a dignified manner or she is a dignitary because of her position in government. But dignity as God sees it is the inherent value and worth you hold because you were created in His image. God cares deeply about how we treat each other. He cares so deeply that He sternly warns us of His judgment and justice when we violate the God-given dignity of others.

> **DIGNITY:** The God-given human condition of having value and worth

In Zechariah 7, the people asked God if they should perform a religious act of mourning. But God read their hearts and asked them whether their fasts and feasts were for God or for themselves. He told them, *"Administer true justice; show mercy and compassion to one another. Do not oppress the widow or the fatherless, the alien or the poor. In your hearts do not think evil of each other"* (vv. 9b-10, NIV). But did they listen? Nope. Verses 11 and 12 tell us the people would not obey God or listen to the prophets. And so God said He wouldn't listen to them any longer and would scatter them among the nations (vv. 13-14).

Now fast forward to the New Testament. Matthew 23 records Jesus' epic takedown of the hypocritical religious leaders. In verse 23 He admonishes the Pharisees, ... *For you tithe mint and dill and cumin, and have neglected the weightier matters of the law: justice and mercy and faithfulness. These you ought to have done, without neglecting the others* (ESV). Just like the people in Zechariah 7, the Pharisees were more interested in religious ritual than in loving people. Jesus tells them in verse 28, *Even so you also outwardly appear righteous to men, but inside you are full of hypocrisy and lawlessness* (NKJV). Ouch!

God doesn't care about religious ritual as much as He desires obedience and justice. Unfortunately, this is a common theme throughout the Old Testament prophets, one God must repeat over and over again. It's really easy to go through the motions and do religious things, but God wants us to show love and mercy to everyone, always. Look at the types of people mentioned in Zechariah 7:10: widows, the fatherless, foreigners, and the poor. These are people who are easy to look down upon or to ignore, even to take advantage of and oppress. They're vulnerable. They don't have the means or ability to defend themselves. They are also people in dire need of help. And like us, they are created in the image of God. So if we, followers of Christ, don't help the helpless, then who will?

God cares about humanity, all people, enough to create us all in His own image. As bearers of God's image, every person should be treated with dignity and respect, no matter what color, economic status, age, sexual orientation, or religion. As we saw from today's reading, some of the harshest criticisms in the Bible are directed towards those who ignored the plights of the weak and needy. Being a witness requires that we recognize the dignity of everyone.

BASED ON THE READING, WRITE A QUESTION YOU MIGHT HAVE.

_____

_____

_____

_____

CORE CONCEPT & VERSES

CORE CONCEPT:
Being a witness requires that I see everyone, always, with dignity and respect.

READ & WRITE THESE VERSES: 1 PETER 2:16-17

Use the space below to help you remember these verses. Feel free to write, draw, or design in ways that make sense to you.

ABOUT THESE VERSES:

Peter designed and wrote his letter to Christians living in Rome and experiencing some intense persecution for believing in Jesus. Yet for Peter, it was the grace of God that would provide sufficient comfort in times of trouble. No matter what the Roman Empire could throw at them, the grace of God found only in Christ would be enough. Much of this letter is focused on the believers' actions towards the rest of the world. In other words, how should people looking in from the outside see the grace of God manifested in the lives of God's people?

This week's verses help us to see that even in the midst of injustice or wrongdoing, believers in Christ ought to continue to persevere in the life God has called each of us to. Freedom is not necessarily freedom from the world's prisons, but the freedom found in Christ. This freedom from the world, freedom from hatred, bitterness, or retribution, is a gift available and intended for every person. Therefore every person is deserving of dignity and respect, regardless of their treatment or actions toward us. That is the grace and love Christ showed toward us.

EXPLORATION QUESTIONS

Choose two questions from below. Spend the next two days exploring them. Feel free to use reference books (like Bible dictionaries, commentaries, concordances), search online, listen to/watch sermons, and/or ask a mentor/parent/pastor. Record your findings below.

☐ 1. What qualities do humans possess that make us worthy of honor and respect?

☐ 2. What warning did God give to those violating the dignity of others?

☐ 3. Where did Jesus model loving and respecting the dignity of others whom religious leaders shunned?

☐ My own question from yesterday

WANT TO KNOW MORE? CHECK OUT THIS BOOK!

Just a Minute: In the Heart of a Child, One Moment ... Can Last Forever, by Wess Stafford
witnesses.awanaym.org/library

> ACTION PLAN

Based on what you have learned over the last five days about what it means to be a witness, create an action plan for yourself. What questions do you still need answered?

Write a verse that reminds you of how to see and treat others.

> NOTES

CITATION TRACK CHECKLIST >> 5.1

- DAYS 1-6
- CORE VERSES   LEADER'S INITIALS   DATE

ARE YOU ON TRACK WITH YOUR BIBLE READING? RECORD WHAT YOU READ HERE:

▶ INTRO EXPERIENCE

Talk to three different people in your life this week and ask them what signs indicate they are sad or hurting. Write down their answers and then answer the question for yourself.

SIGNS THAT I'M HURTING:

Name:

Name:

Name:

Me:

▶ **WATCH THE VIDEO**
WITNESSES.AWANAYM.ORG

> CORE CONTENT ××××××××××××

Read 1 John 3.

Have you ever received or expressed compassion? What did that look like? How did that experience go beyond kindness or sympathy? The word *compassion* originates from the Latin word *compati*, com – "together" and *pati* – "suffer," or "to suffer together." This implies a depth and complexity far greater than feeling sad or being kind. Throughout Scripture God's love is described in the form of compassion and mercy for us (Colossians 3:12, Isaiah 30:18, Psalm 103:13, 2 Corinthians 1:3-4, etc.). Jesus Himself was compassion. He suffered with us. He entered into our suffering and felt our pain. Compassion is an expression of love. It is a supernatural force that moves someone to action. This week's passage is one passage of many in Scripture that describes what it looks like for us to demonstrate God's love through compassion.

> **COMPASSION:** To suffer alongside of or with someone

John's letters all focus on one thing: love. We learn in 1 John 4:8 that *God is love*. And in today's reading from 1 John 3, we are commanded to love each other (v. 11). Loving each other is the evidence in our lives that we have been saved (v. 14). And like everything in the Christian life, it begins with Jesus. We love others because Jesus loved us. John sums up the entire gospel message nicely in verse 23: ... *To believe in the name of His Son, Jesus Christ, and to love one another as He commanded us* (NIV). Thus the core of Christianity can be explained rather simply: love God and love others.

But what does it mean to actually love people? How do we act out this love? So often we treat love like it's just a feeling. But in verses 17 and 18 we learn that love compels us to act. It's one thing to tell someone, "I love you." It's another thing to actually love them, to sacrifice for them, to give your all for them. This is exactly what God did for us when He sent us His Son (John 3:16). Romans 5:8 says that Christ's death for us was a demonstration of His love. In these verses John tells us to show pity and sacrifice what we have for the sake of those in need. John is calling us out here. You can be assured of your love for God when you begin to demonstrate love for others (v. 19).

Loving God and loving others are not two separate things. We love God by loving others. In Matthew 25, Jesus provides a glimpse of the final judgment. He will tell the righteous: ... *I was hungry and you gave Me something to eat, I was thirsty and you gave Me something to drink, I was a stranger and you invited Me in, I needed clothes and you clothed Me, I was sick and you looked after Me, I was in prison and you came to visit Me* (vv. 35-36, NIV). This is because ... *whatever you did for one of the least of these brothers of mine, you did for Me* (v. 40, NIV). So whenever we show compassion towards others, we show compassion to Jesus. However, the opposite is also true, that when we deny compassion towards others, we also deny compassion towards Him (vv. 41-45). That's how much Jesus cares about everyone!

BASED ON THE READING, WRITE A QUESTION YOU MIGHT HAVE.

CORE CONCEPT & VERSES

CORE CONCEPT:
Being a witness requires that I demonstrate love and compassion.

READ & WRITE THESE VERSES: 1 JOHN 3:17-18

Use the space below to help you remember these verses.
Feel free to write, draw, or design in ways that make sense to you.

ABOUT THESE VERSES:

The core of the gospel is love. This is what John makes abundantly clear in his first letter. *God is love.* Christians ought to love one another. And love is much more than feeling, it also requires action. Even if someone claims to love but does not exemplify such love, that person is a liar and Christ is not in him. Love is the willingness to lay one's life down for another, to have compassion for others, and to see what ought to be done for others and acting on it.

The beauty of John's letter is that we get a crystal-clear picture of what it means to follow Jesus—we must walk as He did. The command is not to love in concept only, but in how we act, what we do for others, and how we treat each other. We walk in truth when we walk in love.

▶ EXPLORATION QUESTIONS

Choose two questions from below. Spend the next two days exploring them. Feel free to use reference books (like Bible dictionaries, commentaries, concordances), search online, listen to/watch sermons, and/or ask a mentor/parent/pastor. Record your findings below.

☐ 1. How has God suffered alongside you? Use verses to back up your answer.

☐ 3. How can others know the gospel through our compassionate actions?

☐ 2. How do we also benefit from being compassionate toward others?

☐ My own question from yesterday

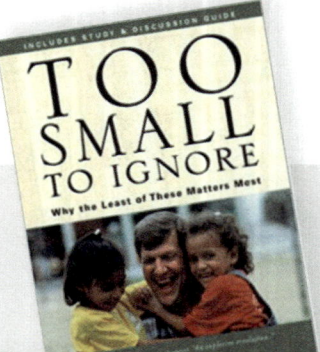

WANT TO KNOW MORE? CHECK OUT THIS BOOK!

Too Small to Ignore: Why the Least of These Matters Most, by Wess Stafford
witnesses.awanaym.org/library

> ACTION PLAN

Based on what you have learned over the last five days about what it means to be a witness, create an action plan for yourself. What questions do you still need answered?

Who is experiencing suffering that you are aware of, and how can you demonstrate love and compassion to them?

> NOTES

CITATION TRACK CHECKLIST >> 5.2

☐ DAYS 1-6
☐ CORE VERSES   LEADER'S INITIALS   DATE

ARE YOU ON TRACK WITH YOUR BIBLE READING? RECORD WHAT YOU READ HERE:

▶ INTRO EXPERIENCE

Imagine you are alone in the lunchroom at school, in line to buy your lunch. You witness a group of older students walk up to a table and begin picking on a younger student. The younger student was not bothering anyone; he was just sitting alone eating his lunch. If you have experienced this, recall an actual experience.

What do you do?

Would your decision change if you were with a group of your friends? Why or why not?

In either case, what motivated your actions?

CORE CONTENT

Read Psalm 82.

In John 9, Jesus heals a blind man on the Sabbath. And like everything else Jesus did, the Pharisees didn't like it. Jesus then used this opportunity to explain to them that He was the Messiah. The Pharisees attempted to stone Him for blasphemy since He claimed to be God, and He responded by quoting a passage from today's reading with: *"Is it not written in your Law, 'I have said you are gods'?"* *(John 10:34, NIV)*; which is a direct quote from today's passage. This seems like an odd thing to say, to call the Pharisees gods. So let's look at Psalm 82 to understand what Jesus meant.

Verses 6 and 7 (NIV) state, *"I said, 'You are "gods"; you are all sons of the Most High.' But you will die like mere men; you will fall like every other ruler."* That last phrase in verse 7, *every other ruler*, leads many scholars to think that "gods" refers to rulers, judges, and other people in authority. But why such a harsh statement to them, that they will die and fall? Verse 2 explains that these rulers defend the unjust and show partiality to the wicked.

But while these "gods" have power and authority on earth, the first and last verses of Psalm 82 remind us that God is the true judge over all creation, and He will ultimately repay the wicked for all of their evil deeds. So what should authorities do instead? *Defend the cause of the weak and the fatherless; maintain the rights of the poor and oppressed. Rescue the weak and the needy; deliver them from the hand of the wicked* (vv. 3-4, NIV).

This is what makes Jesus' criticism of the religious leaders in John 9 and 10 so unfortunate. They should have been experts in the Old Testament Scriptures and thus known exactly what they taught, including Jesus' reference to Psalm 82. The Pharisees criticized Jesus for doing a good work on the Sabbath. Yet they neglected to do truly good works themselves. Instead, they preyed upon the weak to amass power and prestige.

AFFLICTED: One who has been knocked down or weakened by force or illness

The ultimate goal of a witness is obviously to share the gospel. However, this is not all that God requires of us. We need to defend the weak and powerless. Today's Core Verses say: *Speak up for those who cannot speak for themselves, for the rights of all who are destitute. Speak up and judge fairly; defend the rights of the poor and needy (Proverbs 31:8-9, NIV).*

You may ask yourself, "Who am I? What can I really do?" And that's understandable. You may be young. You may not have any position of authority. But you don't have to be some great political revolutionary; you can defend someone being bullied in school. You can volunteer your time, money, influence, or privilege in status to speak up for the dignity and rights of others. Lots of little things can make a big difference. When you defend the weak and powerless, you are being a true witness for Christ.

BASED ON THE READING, WRITE A QUESTION YOU MIGHT HAVE.

_____

_____

_____

_____

CORE CONCEPT & VERSES

CORE CONCEPT:
Being a witness to the helpless requires defending against injustice and amplifying their voice.

READ & WRITE THESE VERSES: PROVERBS 31:8-9

Use the space below to help you remember these verses. Feel free to write, draw, or design in ways that make sense to you.

ABOUT THESE VERSES:

Proverbs 31 is attributed to a king named Lemuel. However, there is no mention of such a king in the historical records of Israel. Some scholars have suggested Lemuel (literally meaning "devoted to God") as a pen name for Solomon, perhaps given by Bathsheba. Others, however, have suggested Lemuel is a foreign king who converted and was a follower of Mosaic law. However, both suggestions have little or no positive evidence and are merely guesses.

What we do know is that the conduct of a godly and wise king was more than military power and prowess or kingdom expansion. The wise king would also be concerned with the welfare of all of those within his kingdom. Under the rule of a wise king, even the poor and oppressed have a voice and will receive fair judgment.

> *EXPLORATION QUESTIONS*

Choose two questions from below. Spend the next two days exploring them. Feel free to use reference books (like Bible dictionaries, commentaries, concordances), search online, listen to/watch sermons, and/or ask a mentor/parent/pastor. Record your findings below.

☐ 1. What were the responsibilities of Israel's rulers whom Psalm 82 was written to, and how had they failed in those responsibilities according to the passage?

☐ 2. Why do you think it's so important to God to defend the weak and helpless?

☐ 3. Who are the weak and needy?

☐ My own question from yesterday

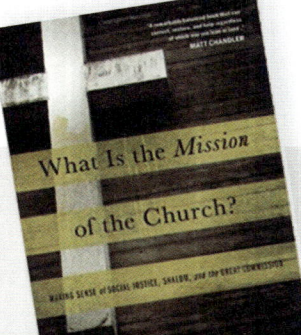

WANT TO KNOW MORE? CHECK OUT THIS BOOK!

What Is the Mission of the Church?, by Kevin DeYoung and Greg Gilbert
by Greg Stier   witnesses.awanaym.org/library

ACTION PLAN

Based on what you have learned over the last five days about what it means to be a witness, create an action plan for yourself. What questions do you still need answered?

Whom do you know that is helpless and how will you defend them?

Hear the voices and stories from kids around the world.
VISIT AWANA.ORG/GOGLOBAL

NOTES

CITATION TRACK CHECKLIST >> 5.3

DAYS 1-6

CORE VERSES   LEADER'S INITIALS   DATE

ARE YOU ON TRACK WITH YOUR BIBLE READING? RECORD WHAT YOU READ HERE:

▸ INTRO EXPERIENCE

Take or draw a picture of a place in which you find comfort and safety.

▸ WATCH THE VIDEO
WITNESSES.AWANAYM.ORG

CORE CONTENT ✕ ✕ ✕ ✕ ✕ ✕ ✕ ✕ ✕ ✕ ✕

Read Psalm 36.

Many colleges nowadays are creating safe spaces on campus, locations where students are sheltered from abuse and offensive ideas. But did you know that the church was the original safe space? The main worship area of a church building is called a sanctuary, which literally means "a sacred place." But the meaning of the word *sanctuary* in everyday language has been expanded to mean "a safe place." Throughout history, churches were political refuges, places where criminals could not be arrested. Hence a *sanctuary*, or safe place.

REFUGE: A place of safety, shelter, and protection; a sanctuary

This should not surprise us, as throughout the Bible, God is constantly called our refuge: *The LORD is my rock and my fortress and my deliverer; my God, my strength, in whom I will trust; my shield and the horn of my salvation, my stronghold (Psalm 18:2, NKJV). God is our refuge and strength, an ever-present help in trouble. Therefore we will not fear, though the earth give way and the mountains fall into the heart of the sea, though its waters roar and foam and the mountains quake with their surging (Psalm 46:1-3, NIV)*. And from today's reading: *How precious is your steadfast love, O God! The children of mankind take refuge in the shadow of Your wings. They feast on the abundance of Your house, and You give them drink from the river of Your delights. For with You is the fountain of life; in Your light do we see light (Psalm 36:7-9, ESV)*.

Many of the Psalms were written by David, who relied heavily on God as his refuge. His life was in danger many times and he constantly cried out to God to save him from his enemies. And God was always faithful.

Now you may not be at risk of physical danger. But God can be your refuge in other ways. Jesus said, *"Come to Me, all you who labor and are heavy laden, and I will give you rest. Take My yoke upon you and learn from Me, for I am gentle and lowly in heart, and you will find rest for your souls. For My yoke is easy and My burden is light" (Matthew 11:28-30, NKJV)*.

But what about when we mess up and are the source of our own trouble? Psalm 103:8 says: *The LORD is compassionate and gracious, slow to anger, abounding in love* (NIV). When we make mistakes, we need to run *to* God, not *from* Him. Think about the father in the story of the prodigal son. He waited for his son to return to him and welcomed him with open arms. Likewise, when we mess up, God waits for us patiently, ready to forgive us and to comfort us.

You may also face hardships and persecution because you are a witness for Christ. In America, you may be mocked and called names. In other countries, you could be imprisoned or even put to death. But do not fear, because the Lord is always your refuge and strength:

The LORD is my light and my salvation; whom shall I fear? The LORD is the stronghold of my life; of whom shall I be afraid? (Psalm 27:1, ESV).

BASED ON THE READING, WRITE A QUESTION YOU MIGHT HAVE.

CORE CONCEPT & VERSES

CORE CONCEPT:
Refuge and shelter can be found in God alone, no matter what the circumstance.

READ & WRITE THESE VERSES: PSALM 36:7-9

Use the space below to help you remember these verses. Feel free to write, draw, or design in ways that make sense to you.

ABOUT THESE VERSES

Psalm 36 is set against the backdrop of the evil deeds and schemes of men. David, the servant of the Lord, expresses confidence and praise in light of God's character and protection. David can be sure of salvation from his enemies because of God's protective love. The world may not fear God and His judgment and will continue to pursue evil. However, David's perspective presents an alternative of resting in God almighty and the essentials of a balanced life in Christ.

This week's passage emphasizes the power and peace of resting under the wings of the Almighty. Despite David's trouble and tribulation, he is always reminded that true peace and refuge can only be found in God. Only in Christ can light be found. Only in Christ can the kingdom of heaven manifest itself on earth.

▶ EXPLORATION QUESTIONS

Choose two questions from below. Spend the next two days exploring them. Feel free to use reference books (like Bible dictionaries, commentaries, concordances), search online, listen to/watch sermons, and/or ask a mentor/parent/pastor. Record your findings below.

☐ 1. What Scripture passage encourages you most in the safety and refuge found in God alone?

☐ 2. How does the Bible describe the way to take refuge in God?

☐ 3. How has God been a refuge in your life?

☐ My own question from yesterday

WANT TO KNOW MORE? CHECK OUT THIS BOOK!

Slow Kingdom Coming: Practices for Doing Justice, Loving Mercy and Walking Humbly in the World, by Kent Annan witnesses.awanaym.org/library

▶ ACTION PLAN

Based on what you have learned over the last five days about what it means to be a witness, create an action plan for yourself. What questions do you still need answered?

Name an area of your life in which you need God's protection and safety.

▶ NOTES

CITATION TRACK CHECKLIST >> 5.4

DAYS 1-6

CORE VERSES   LEADER'S INITIALS   DATE

ARE YOU ON TRACK WITH YOUR BIBLE READING? RECORD WHAT YOU READ HERE:

 **WATCH THE VIDEO**
awanaym.org/videos

GIFTS
UNIT 06

Hey friends,

How packed was the last unit, am I right?! So much good stuff! One of my biggest takeaways was that receiving and giving are intricately connected. Talking with experts in Uganda, we learned that we must first recognize our personal dignity before we can recognize the dignity of others. Only by starting with ourselves can our eyes then recognize the dignity in other people.

Connecting with others makes us care. And caring moves us to action. The more we care, the more we are compelled to action. In my talk with Kawesa, he said that we strengthen our ability to fight for others when we tap into and explore our God-given gifts. Sweet! But then we have to ask, what are my gifts? And how can I find my own way to share the gospel and speak up for the silenced?

It is more blessed to give than it is to receive (see Acts 20:35). There's something to be said about the blessings that we receive when we give ourselves away to lifting others up. We gain peace, joy, and satisfaction in serving. But just as true is the discovery of talents, passions, and interests that we uncover when we serve.

To get more on this, I made my way to Hawaii (I know, I seriously took one for the team!) and met with the spoken word artist and author, Jefferson Bethke. He opened up about his story and the creative forms that he has found in sharing about Jesus. Bethke has been one of my favorite artists, speakers, authors, and figures on YouTube® for years! His words both inspired and nurtured my growth as I transitioned into a relationship with Jesus.

As we talked, he shared about the intentional diversity that God implemented in our design, and that we are individually and uniquely created on purpose. In a way, we know this truth. But we certainly don't always own it. Bethke reminded us that we share a responsibility to use this given uniqueness for His wonderful glory!

So as you dive into this unit, I encourage you to do a little soul-searching, because this unit is 100% yours. What is it that you are good at, and is the most exciting while doing? Think about how to tap into those things for His glory. Combining your passions with your love for God may look like nothing you've seen before, and that may be exactly what God was aiming for.

Your co-adventurer,

Kelly Carolini

▶ INTRO EXPERIENCE

Create a self-portrait using any medium you prefer. Be creative and use your unique gifts. You could use pen, paints, clay, music, code, or even baking ingredients.

▶ WATCH THE VIDEO
WITNESSES.AWANAYM.ORG

CORE CONTENT

Read Genesis 1.

"There is no such thing as a new idea." When Mark Twain penned those words he followed it up by saying that we instead continually take old ideas and repackage them into new combinations of thought that resemble something new. Similarly, the writer of Ecclesiastes wrote, ... *There is nothing new under the sun. (Ecclesiastes 1:9*, NKJV). It almost seems obvious that we are on a constant cycle of repeat. Many philosophers believe the concept of an original idea is nothing more than a myth or only our perception of originality. In many ways this idea is true. Whether it is our stories, our inventions, or even our ideas, we can point to several similarities. However, what might seem like a lack of originality only appears so because all of our thoughts and ideas stem from one common source—God.

In Genesis 1 we see the creativity of God on full display in His creation of the universe from nothing. God made the sun and moon, the land and sea, the birds and fish—all unique and special. All of it was designed with special intent and purpose. But most importantly, God uniquely created humanity. After each day of creation—every time God created something new and unique—He declared it good. In English the word *good* doesn't carry much excitement. But in Hebrew the word carries a slightly nuanced and therefore more significant meaning—it pronounces that everything is right, or just as it should be. In other words, it is like that feeling of excitement and satisfaction of playing a piece of music perfectly, or scoring the game-winning goal. In that moment, everything is just as it ought to be. But after the sixth day, when God created humanity, He said it was *very good*.

The creation of humanity on day six is the climax of creation—it was more than just satisfying or just as it should be, it was exceedingly good. Humanity would be the prize of creation, valued more than anything else, commanded to rule and have dominion over the rest of creation. But why did God place such an emphasis and importance on humanity? Why place us in higher esteem than the rest of creation? God's desire for humanity was that we would be set apart from everything else and that we would bear His divine image. Although imperfect, finite, and now tainted, each person has in them attributes of God—things like a sense of justice, personality, wisdom, love, and the ability to create. The rest of creation, although beautifully created to be good, would be placed a step below humanity.

Although our thoughts and actions may not be completely unique in every conceivable way, as divine image bearers we are, in fact, incredibly unique. Even science has confirmed what Scripture has already affirmed—every part of us, down to the wiring of our brains, is different from one another. Each one of us is an original thought of God designed to reflect the originality of God. Who God has made you to be is exactly who He wants you to be. The uniqueness of you is exactly how God intended for the gospel to make it to the ends of the earth. It is just as Oscar Wilde has been credited with saying, "Be yourself. Everyone else is taken."

> ***IMAGO DEI*:** Latin for image of God, a doctrine or theological concept which describes the human condition as being made in the image of God (Genesis 1:27)

BASED ON THE READING, WRITE A QUESTION YOU MIGHT HAVE.

CORE CONCEPT & VERSE

CORE CONCEPT:
As image bearers of God, we have been created uniquely.

READ & WRITE THIS VERSE: GENESIS 1:27

Use the space below to help you remember this verse.
Feel free to write, draw, or design in ways that make sense to you.

ABOUT THIS VERSE:

God created. It is how the entire story of God begins, with a detailed description of God's creative nature making all there is. The first chapter in Genesis is designed to introduce us to not only God and His creation, but it is designed to introduce us to humanity. This introduction is vital to how we come to understand the nature of the gospel and our salvation in Christ. Like any great story, we are given a glimpse, though only for a moment, of God's unique and special creation, built just as He intended.

The text of Genesis takes special care to be clear that humanity is set apart from the rest of creation. The flow of Chapter 1 almost seems to rush through the rest of creation in order to get to humanity. God wants to make certain that we understand our origin and unique design—that we are created in His image.

EXPLORATION QUESTIONS

Choose two questions from below. Spend the next two days exploring them. Feel free to use reference books (like Bible dictionaries, commentaries, concordances), search online, listen to/watch sermons, and/or ask a mentor/parent/pastor. Record your findings below.

- [ ] 1. How does Scripture describe humankind and how are we a reflection of God?
- [ ] 2. How is the character of God an encouragement for us to be creative?
- [ ] 3. Do we have a responsibility to create things for His glory? Why or why not?
- [ ] My own question from yesterday

WANT TO KNOW MORE? CHECK OUT THIS BOOK!

The Artisan Soul: Crafting Your Life into a Work of Art, by Erwin Raphael McManus
witnesses.awanaym.org/library

▶ ACTION PLAN

Based on what you have learned over the last five days about what it means to be a witness, create an action plan for yourself. What questions do you still need answered?

List the ways you have been created uniquely. How are those things a reflection of God?

▶ NOTES

CITATION TRACK CHECKLIST >> 6.1

☐ DAYS 1-6
☐ CORE VERSES   LEADER'S INITIALS   DATE

ARE YOU ON TRACK WITH YOUR BIBLE READING? RECORD WHAT YOU READ HERE:

INTRO EXPERIENCE

Have you ever modified something to make it better or unique to your own style? Maybe you've doodled art on your notebook or backpack, decked out a skateboard or sports gear, or even mashed up some images and videos.

Take something that you already have and modify it to create something new or better as an act of worship or honor to God. Bring your new creation to show your group.

IF HELPFUL, USE THE SPACE BELOW TO PLAN.

 WATCH THE VIDEO
WITNESSES.AWANAYM.ORG

CORE CONTENT

Read Genesis 2.

If all God had done was create us, it would have been enough. If all God had done was create us in His own image, uniquely designed, each as an original thought of a divine mind, that, too, would have been enough. But instead, God went even farther. He created us to be productive and left us in charge. Even at the very beginning God knew there would be a need for civilizations, technology, art, music, and literature. God knew there would be a need for scientists, mathematicians, lawyers, doctors, teachers, and construction workers. God knew there would be a need, because He wanted His image to be reflected in not only all that He created, but in all that we create as well.

As image bearers of the divine Creator, we have been created to create. God's command to Adam after everything had been created was to have dominion over all creation, give every animal and creature a name, to care for the garden of Eden, and once Eve joined him to be fruitful and multiply. This is known as the Creation Mandate. It is a mandate that compels humanity to do more than just exist and use God's creation. It is a mandate to work alongside of God as co-laborers and co-creators. God has given us the canvas and given each of us the divine command to craft in ways that glorify Him and His image in us. He commanded us to cultivate creation.

CULTIVATE: Work done to prepare, acquire, or develop something

For Adam cultivating meant literally working the ground. God provided creation's first parents with everything they needed to care for the earth, multiply, create technology, etc., so that all of creation would reflect back to God. Today, although we are not all working the ground like Adam, we each have been given a craft to cultivate specifically to glorify the Creator. This is precisely what God was talking about in Genesis 1:26 and 2:15.

All of us have been created to create. Even if you don't consider yourself a creative person—you are. Even if you are not musically inclined but are a math wizard—you are creative. With the correct mathematical formula and the right points plotted on a graph, math can create a three-dimensional heart—or any object for that matter. Lawyers take evidence and information to create arguments. Accountants might look at a household or company budget and create possible solutions for greater financial health. Engineers create working systems—whether buildings, technology, or even chemical formulas.

Witnesses for the gospel do far more than just talk about Jesus. Witnesses use the gifts, abilities, talents, and desires—their entire lives—in order to create something that points back to and reflects the glory of God. Being a witness is about taking who God made us to be and using it to show who He is. Not only are we each a unique, original thought of God, but also each of us has been specifically built as a co-creator charged with the divine responsibility to proclaim the name of Jesus and the power of the gospel.

BASED ON THE READING, WRITE A QUESTION YOU MIGHT HAVE.

CORE CONCEPT & VERSE

CORE CONCEPT:
As image bearers of God, we have been created to create.

READ & WRITE THIS VERSE: GENESIS 2:15

Use the space below to help you remember this verse. Feel free to write, draw, or design in ways that make sense to you.

ABOUT THE VERSE

The focus from Genesis 1 to Genesis 2 shifts from introducing God, His creation, and the prize of creation humanity, to the instructions given to humanity. But because humans were created in the image of God, our purpose must also reflect that image. This is often called the Creation Mandate. From the very beginning God intended for humanity to be co-creators and co-laborers in overseeing creation.

However, the idea of work in the garden does not mean endless toil of the same mundane routine. It is descriptive of the creative work humanity is called to. This verse sets the stage for humanity as sub-creators in everything we do as a reflection of who God is.

▶ EXPLORATION QUESTIONS

Choose two questions from below. Spend the next two days exploring them. Feel free to use reference books (like Bible dictionaries, commentaries, concordances), search online, listen to/watch sermons, and/or ask a mentor/parent/pastor. Record your findings below.

☐ 1. Where in the Bible (not only in Genesis) has God given us a responsibility to be creative?

☐ 2. Who is a great example of being faithful in productivity and creativity in the Bible? Why?

☐ 3. In what ways are you creative and productive?

☐ My own question from yesterday

WANT TO KNOW MORE? CHECK OUT THIS BOOK!

Culture Making: Recovering Our Creative Calling, by Andy Crouch
witnesses.awanaym.org/library

▶ ACTION PLAN

Based on what you have learned over the last five days about what it means to be a witness, create an action plan for yourself. What questions do you still need answered?

What will you create as a reflection of God this week?

▶ NOTES

CITATION TRACK CHECKLIST >> 6.2

DAYS 1-6

CORE VERSES   LEADER'S INITIALS   DATE

ARE YOU ON TRACK WITH YOUR BIBLE READING? RECORD WHAT YOU READ HERE:

INTRO EXPERIENCE

Take an inventory. Look in your bedroom and list all of the things that you have in your room that haven't been used in the last three months.

- [ ]
- [ ]
- [ ]
- [ ]
- [ ]
- [ ]
- [ ]
- [ ]
- [ ]
- [ ]
- [ ]
- [ ]
- [ ]
- [ ]
- [ ]

WATCH THE VIDEO
WITNESSES.AWANAYM.ORG

CORE CONTENT

Read Matthew 25:14-30.

You have been created in the divine image. In that likeness, you also have been given the ability to reflect that image with what you create. But this image we possess is not a privilege, it is a responsibility. This image we hold is not something that can be neglected, or buried, or altogether ignored. The Creation Mandate given to Adam was more than just a task to complete, but a dedication to God of everything Adam was given as an act of worship. The mandate applies to us in the same way. Jesus makes this point clear in today's reading.

> **FAITHFULNESS:** Being diligent and loyal to the work for which God designed you

Look at how Jesus describes how the master responded to his three servants. The two who invested the talents entrusted to them were rewarded, while the master took back from the one who was afraid and hid his talents. Why was the master so angry with the foolish servant who hid the talent allotted to him? The money given to each servant had much potential. When hidden and buried, the one talent was not only wasted, but actually cost the master much in potential gains. In return the foolish servant lost everything he was given and any hope for future blessing.

Although this story is about money, the point of Jesus' parable is caring for what God has entrusted us with. Those who take care of and invest what they are given will be given more, but those who neglect or ignore what has been entrusted to them will lose what they have. Whether you prefer to quote Voltaire or Uncle Ben Parker from Spider-Man, both make Jesus' point: "With great power comes great responsibility." This is a story about stewardship and we are therefore called to be stewards of our divine image.

Because we are uniquely designed specifically by God and for God, we have the responsibility to recognize and refine our gifts, talents, and abilities, working to become more like Christ with every step and reflecting Him in more significant ways. But it is more than just recognizing our unique gifts and talents, or even honing those gifts and talents in hopes of honoring God in some way. There is great power in what God has given us because those gifts and talents are the means by which God can use us to change the trajectory of someone else's life and bring them back to Him. Our gifts and talents are the mechanisms or wiring for how each of us can best communicate the gospel and be a witness for Christ.

Think about who God has made you to be, what you love to do, and what you love to create. Think about how you can uniquely point others to Christ. Just like the servants in this week's passage, our Lord, our Father, has entrusted us with something of great value that holds infinite potential if we use and invest it faithfully. In the same way, Paul urges Timothy not to neglect his gifts (1 Timothy 4:14), to read the Scripture publicly, to preach, and to teach .Be bold and diligent in your efforts to move the gospel forward and let others see Christ through your gifts and abilities.

BASED ON THE READING, WRITE A QUESTION YOU MIGHT HAVE.

- -

- -

- -

- -

CORE CONCEPT & VERSE

CORE CONCEPT:
We are called to steward the abilities, resources, and opportunities God provides.

READ & WRITE THIS VERSE: 1 TIMOTHY 4:14

Use the space below to help you remember this verse.
Feel free to write, draw, or design in ways that make sense to you.

ABOUT THIS VERSE:

After spending several years with Paul as his travel companion, Timothy was commissioned with leading the church in Ephesus. Paul's first letter to Timothy was meant to provide the church with crystal clear direction for how to establish leadership within the local church and keeping the message of the gospel at the center. It was not uncommon for the church to be infiltrated and influenced by others with a different message or a different gospel.

This letter gives us a glimpse at what it means and what is required of Christian leadership. Timothy was called to model the ideal Christlike behavior. As a leader it was Timothy's responsibility to use his gifts as well as the gifts of others in order to further the ministry and guide others to following Christ.

▶ EXPLORATION QUESTIONS

Choose two questions from below. Spend the next two days exploring them. Feel free to use reference books (like Bible dictionaries, commentaries, concordances), search online, listen to/watch sermons, and/or ask a mentor/parent/pastor. Record your findings below.

☐ 1. How would you describe the two servants with whom the master was pleased?

☐ 2. How did the master respond to each servant when he returned?

☐ 3. In verse 23 the master says, *"Well done, good and faithful servant ..."* What did they do to be called faithful and how does this challenge or encourage you?

☐ My own question from yesterday

WANT TO KNOW MORE? CHECK OUT THIS BOOK!

The Imagination of God: Art, Creativity and Truth in the Bible, by Brian Godawa
witnesses.awanaym.org/library

▶ ACTION PLAN

Based on what you have learned over the last five days about what it means to be a witness, create an action plan for yourself. What questions do you still need answered? List any areas of your life you need to steward better to honor God.

MY PLAN

MY LIST

▶ NOTES

CITATION TRACK CHECKLIST >> 6.3

DAYS 1-6

CORE VERSES   LEADER'S INITIALS   DATE

ARE YOU ON TRACK WITH YOUR BIBLE READING? RECORD WHAT YOU READ HERE:

▶ INTRO EXPERIENCE

Find a piece of art: a song, a piece of literature, a painting, etc.

How is this piece of art a reflection of the artist?

What message is the art piece communicating?

WITNESSES.AWANAYM.ORG

CORE CONTENT

Read Colossians 3:1-11, 1 Timothy 4:6-16.

No matter what you do, what you are good at, or what your talents are, you can always do it better. Every musician, artist, athlete, business professional, or teacher knows practice is the only path to an improved, polished presentation. It is as though God did not finish the job when He created you—He was just getting started. His goal is that you—His canvas—look increasingly more and more like Christ. Every experience, every relationship, and every activity is a new brushstroke on your blank canvas. Declaring your faith in Christ does not end with your verbal confession of Christ as Lord. It is only the beginning.

All through his letters, Paul constantly reminds his readers that to be a Christian is to be a new creation—constantly shedding the old, sinful life and being refined into someone more resembling Christ. This advice stems from his own experience (Acts 9). Specifically, in his letter to the Colossian church, Paul reminds this young group of believers that Christ is not just part of their lives, but the center (3:4). He is the subject of our living masterpiece. But this doesn't mean that we become perfectly sinless once we accept Christ, but with practice we can become more like Him.

Paul gives a list of sinful activities that Christians must actively put to death (3:5). No longer are they to act as the world does: instead they are to take off their old self with its bad practices and put on a new self (3:9-10). Paul is reminding the Colossians that they are an unfinished canvas, daily being made more and more to look and act like Christ. So if their goal is to be true followers of Christ, they need to imitate His example of love and holiness.

> **RENEWAL:** Ridding of something old and worn out and replacing it with something new

But just like any great work of art, it is meant to be displayed and admired, not hidden away. Jesus told the disciples that the kingdom was designed to be a city on a hill, a shining lamp for everyone to see, take notice of, and serve as a guide in the darkness (Matthew 5:14). Our lives as followers of Jesus should bear witness to the gospel at work in us. The gospel has incredible transformative power because of the power of the Spirit at work. But the only way people can take notice, admire Him, follow His light, or hear His music, is by us showing off our new selves—by clothing ourselves *with compassion, kindness, humility, gentleness and patience* (3:12, NIV). We must be people of forgiveness, love, and unity. We must be people that show off God's amazing work of art.

But how? How can we shed our lust, our anger, our lies? How do we put on our new selves? In one sense, we already have. We were *raised with Christ* (v. 1), and so we are made new. Sometimes we just need to remind ourselves of that! "I'm a new person. That old, sinful person is gone." But the new self is also *being renewed in knowledge in the image of its Creator* (v. 10, NIV). When we study the Bible and learn about God, we aren't merely amassing information about our Maker; we are becoming more like Him.

BASED ON THE READING, WRITE A QUESTION YOU MIGHT HAVE.

CORE CONCEPT & VERSE

CORE CONCEPT:
Our lives bear witness to the gospel at work in us.

READ & WRITE THIS VERSE: COLOSSIANS 3:10

Use the space below to help you remember this verse. Feel free to write, draw, or design in ways that make sense to you.

ABOUT THE VERSE

The church in the city of Colossae was largely Gentile, yet suffered from a strange influence of false doctrines coming from Old Testament Jewish roots mixed with pagan philosophy. This created two unique but important problems for the Colossian church. One problem dealt with combining legalism with Christianity based in the grace and finished work of Jesus. The second combined mystical philosophies with faith in Christ. This, of course, led to behaviors and practices inconsistent with Jesus' life and teachings.

Paul's call to the Colossians was to rid themselves of this skewed way of thinking and all that it creates and become someone new. It was a call to recognize the supremacy of Christ as well as the power they possessed as followers and witnesses of Him.

▶ EXPLORATION QUESTIONS

Choose two questions from below. Spend the next two days exploring them. Feel free to use reference books (like Bible dictionaries, commentaries, concordances), search online, listen to/watch sermons, and/or ask a mentor/parent/pastor. Record your findings below.

☐ 1. What imagery does Paul use in vv. 1-4 to describe what happens to our sin?

☐ 2. Describe a new creation in Christ according to this week's passage.

☐ 3. What message is your life sharing with the world?

☐ My own question from yesterday

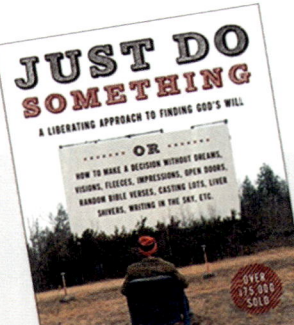

WANT TO KNOW MORE? CHECK OUT THIS BOOK!

Just Do Something: A Liberating Approach to Finding God's Will, by Kevin DeYoung
witnesses.awanaym.org/library

ACTION PLAN

Based on what you have learned over the last five days about what it means to be a witness, create an action plan for yourself. What questions do you still need answered?

How will you show the world you're a new creation this week?

NOTES

CITATION TRACK CHECKLIST >> 6.4

- DAYS 1-6
- CORE VERSES

LEADER'S INITIALS

DATE

ARE YOU ON TRACK WITH YOUR BIBLE READING? RECORD WHAT YOU READ HERE:

 **WATCH THE VIDEO**
awanaym.org/videos

CHALLENGES
UNIT 07

Hey friends,

So how did it go? Did you uncover a bunch of your gifts in the last unit? Did you figure out how you want to use them to share the gospel? If you did, that's great! These things usually take time. By now, you may have tried a few new ways to witness to others. Best-case scenario, you've had some great experiences. Worst-case scenario, you learned something valuable. But even if your efforts were ignored or rejected, this happens And it can be easy to get discouraged. But God warns and even promises that following Him comes with challenges here and there, and a little bit everywhere else too. Learning to stay rooted and constant despite the blows is the goal of every Christian.

So I reached out to Amy Williams, aka the Hope Dealer, in Chicago. This woman faces on a regular basis unbelievable hardships in her mission to love, care for, and advocate for teens in need of grace and change. And yet her nickname says it all, she is the Hope Dealer. It makes you wonder. How can you get knocked down so many times and still have the hope and fire to continue living and witnessing for Christ?

Here's the thing. Fear is real. It can paralyze you from moving in any direction, even when you want to. And it has solid timing too. The moment you get a vision for your life and find a way for you to best serve God, boom, cue fear. There's fear of failing, being rejected, or possibly both. Amy tackled these doubts. Her ideas challenged my vision in difficult times and perhaps they'll challenge yours too.

So think now about what you are willing to give up to be a witness. Because being one will require some discomfort and sacrifice along the way. In those moments, remember why you share the truth of Christ and what that has done for you. Think about what stops you from sharing the good news you've come to know. Do you know how to push through your fear or respond to those who try to discourage you, or twist your words? Talk to friends in your group and your leader, then write down a statement of commitment by the end of this unit and post it someplace where you'll see it often. This is supposed to be hard, but you have the power of a mighty God within you, so I know this is possible. Do you?

Your co-adventurer,

Kelly Carolini

> *INTRO EXPERIENCE*

What is a childhood fear you had that you later learned was unreasonable?

Did a parent or guardian give you wise words to comfort you? If so, what were they?

How did you overcome your fear?

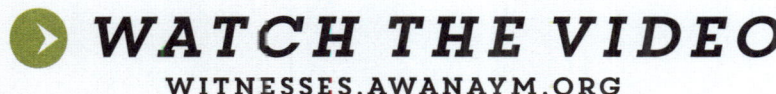

CORE CONTENT

Read Luke 22:54-61.

In his first inaugural address, Franklin D. Roosevelt famously said, "… The only thing to fear is fear itself." Master Yoda warns young Anakin that fear is the path to the dark side. Fear is an extremely powerful emotion that can overcome and paralyze us. And fear can hinder us from being witnesses.

> **DENIAL:** A refusal to accept a truth or reality in order to avoid a negative feeling or action

Peter was one of Jesus' disciples and closest friends. He had promised Jesus he would always follow Him, even if that led to his imprisonment or death (Luke 22:33). Despite Peter's sincerity, such a task would not come easy. After Jesus had been arrested, Peter was overcome by fear and denied that he knew Jesus. Then the text says Jesus looked at Peter, and Peter remembered that Jesus foretold he would deny Him (v. 61). In that moment Peter came face-to-face not only with his fear, but with the power fear had over him.

Why was Peter so afraid, especially after just committing to be there for Jesus? He was part of Jesus' inner circle, traveling with Him for three years. Peter witnessed Jesus' amazing miracles and teachings firsthand. And when Jesus could use his support the most, Peter abandoned Him.

We shouldn't be so hard on Peter. Naturally, Peter would have been afraid of the horror of crucifixion. But in first-century Israel, death was incredibly scary. Without the resurrection of Jesus, it was inconceivable for death to result in a benefit or rescue. For them, it was just darkness and the unknown. All they knew was that they wanted God to be with them. After the resurrection, we can now be assured that the fear of the finality of death has been removed.

How many times have you shied away from sharing the gospel with someone? Maybe you were afraid they would reject you or even mock you. We have all been in that position before. We've all missed out on that perfect opportunity to witness for Christ just because we were afraid of how the other person might respond. And in some countries around the world, sharing the gospel could get you thrown in jail or even killed.

However, let us not forget what Jesus told His disciples about fear: *And do not fear those who kill the body but cannot kill the soul. Rather fear Him who can destroy both soul and body in hell* (Matthew 10:28, ESV).

During Jesus' crucifixion, Peter and many other disciples were nowhere to be found. But when we read about Peter in the book of Acts, he is out fearlessly proclaiming the gospel. What happened? What caused such a drastic change in Peter? The resurrection. When Jesus rose from the dead, He conquered death once and for all. Peter and the disciples had nothing to fear since, even if they were harmed or killed for the gospel, they knew they would spend eternity with Christ. And history teaches us that many of the disciples were, in fact, persecuted and killed for their faith.

The Bible guarantees that we will suffer for the sake of the gospel. Jesus suffered. The disciples suffered. Christians throughout the world continue to suffer for the sake of the gospel. But we should not fear. Jesus defeated sin and death when He rose from the dead. Death is not final. What confidence should this give us in the face of other fears?

BASED ON THE READING, WRITE A QUESTION YOU MIGHT HAVE.

CORE CONCEPT & VERSE

CORE CONCEPT:
We have no reason to fear going where God has called us to go.

READ & WRITE THIS VERSE: PROVERBS 29:25

Use the space below to help you remember this verse. Feel free to write, draw, or design in ways that make sense to you.

ABOUT THIS VERSE:

Proverbs 29 is part of a collection of proverbs gathered by Hezekiah's men about 250 years after Solomon wrote them. These men were charged with copying and grouping them into what we currently possess in the Old Testament. Specifically, Chapter 29 raises the concern and impact fear can have on a person and their judgment, versus trust in God.

The word *fear* used in this context is not the same as fearing God. The fear described here is the kind of fear that intimidates people and allows their actions to be controlled by fear. The wise alternative is trusting in the Lord to drive fear out and there we will find safety and security.

EXPLORATION QUESTIONS

Choose two questions from below. Spend the next two days exploring them. Feel free to use reference books (like Bible dictionaries, commentaries, concordances), search online, listen to/watch sermons, and/or ask a mentor/parent/pastor. Record your findings below.

☐ 1. What would make Peter fearful and deny Jesus? (See Mark 14:55-64.)

☐ 2. Peter often had reason to fear throughout Jesus' ministry on earth. Where else did Jesus patiently teach Peter not to fear?

☐ 3. Despite Peter's fear and impulsiveness, Jesus still acknowledged his ministry as a leader. How did Jesus restore Peter as a leader in Matthew 16 and John 21:15-17?

☐ My own question from yesterday

WANT TO KNOW MORE? CHECK OUT THIS BOOK!

Undaunted: Daring to do what God calls you to do, by Christine Caine
witnesses.awanaym.org/library

▸ ACTION PLAN

Based on what you have learned over the last five days about what it means to be a witness, create an action plan for yourself. What questions do you still need answered?

What fears do you need to release about sharing your faith?

▸ NOTES

CITATION TRACK CHECKLIST >> 7.1

DAYS 1-6

CORE VERSES   LEADER'S INITIALS   DATE

ARE YOU ON TRACK WITH YOUR BIBLE READING? RECORD WHAT YOU READ HERE:

INTRO EXPERIENCE

Send a message to someone who has suffered or has been punished for doing the right thing. Use Scripture to encourage them and remind them of God's love and provision in times of trouble. Record your message and your friend's response in the space below.

WATCH THE VIDEO
WITNESSES.AWANAYM.ORG

CORE CONTENT ××××××××××××

Read Matthew 5:1-12.

Today's reading is from Jesus' famous Sermon on the Mount, most specifically what is known as the Beatitudes (named for the Latin word *beatus*, which means "blessed"). Each verse follows a similar, proverb-like pattern and teaches about those who will be blessed by God: *the poor in spirit* will inherit the kingdom of God (v. 3), those who mourn will be comforted (v. 4), and so on. Verses 10 through 12 end the Beatitudes by discussing the theme for today's lesson: persecution.

Verse 10 states, *Blessed are those who are persecuted for righteousness' sake, for theirs is the kingdom of heaven* (ESV) (which, interestingly, is the same reward for *the poor in spirit* from verse 3). The next two verses continue the theme by including those who are insulted, mistreated, accused falsely of things because of their faith in Christ, and doing God's work. Verses 11-12 call us to rejoice and be glad because our reward is in heaven and others have faced the same horrible treatment before us.

Did Jesus really tell His followers to rejoice in their sufferings? Yes, as this is proof that they are doing God's work. There are many prosperity preachers who teach that God blesses the faithful with health and wealth. But this is outright false. Jesus wasn't rich or famous. He died a criminal's death. All of His disciples suffered, many dying penniless and as martyrs. And this is exactly as Jesus foretold: *"… You will be handed over to be persecuted and put to death, and you will be hated by all nations because of Me"* (Matthew 24:9, NIV).

We read something similar in John 15. Jesus told His disciples: *If the world hates you, keep in mind that it hated Me first* (v. 18) and *If they persecuted Me, they will persecute you also* (v. 20, NIV). 2 Timothy 3:12 says, *… Everyone who wants to live a godly life in Christ Jesus will be persecuted* (NIV). Persecution is guaranteed for anyone who wishes to follow Christ.

This theme recurs throughout the New Testament letters. 1 Peter is an entire letter about facing persecution. Verses 4:13 and 14 state: *But rejoice insofar as you share Christ's sufferings, that you may also rejoice and be glad when His glory is revealed. If you are insulted for the name of Christ, you are blessed, because the Spirit of glory[and of God rests upon you* (ESV). Again, Christians are called to rejoice in their sufferings. Why? It is proof that the Spirit of God is in them.

> **BEATITUDES:** Jesus's sermon found in Matthew 5, named for the Latin word *beatus*, meaning "blessed" or "happy"

The Beatitudes are more than a list of good things Christians should do. They are an assurance that if we suffer for being Christians, it will be worth it. Those who realize their brokenness and need of God's help will receive it (v. 3). Those who do not fight to get ahead, who do not aggressively seek advancement and position, will ultimately receive the entire earth as their reward (v. 5). Jesus promised that although we may face hardships in this life, we will be blessed by God, not necessarily through tangible things like a nice house and car, but through the peace only He can provide. And ultimately, in the next life, we will reign with Him forever.

BASED ON THE READING, WRITE A QUESTION YOU MIGHT HAVE.

CORE CONCEPT & VERSES

CORE CONCEPT:
Jesus promised persecution, but He also promised blessing in our persecution.

READ & WRITE THESE VERSES: MATTHEW 5:11-12

Use the space below to help you remember these verses. Feel free to write, draw, or design in ways that make sense to you.

ABOUT THESE VERSES:

At the beginning of the famous Sermon on the Mount, we are introduced to what is commonly known as the Beatitudes. Those most captivated by the message of Jesus were those Jesus called blessed. The first 11 verses of Chapter 5 introduce what it means and how it means to be blessed. Nine times Jesus repeats, *Blessed are …* The idea of blessing in this context is speaking of the promise of God to care for those who earnestly seek after Him. It is an invitation to enter into the grace that God offers.

Verses 11 and 12 wrap up this section with a sobering reminder that even though the Messiah has come, persecution is still very much a reality. The verses in Chapter 5 leading up to 11 and 12 point to current reality, whereas verses 11 and 12 speak of the near future. The Beatitudes point to the counterculutral reality of the Christian life, but also encourage the imitation of Christ in the midst of inevitable suffering.

▶ EXPLORATION QUESTIONS

Choose two questions from below. Spend the next two days exploring them. Feel free to use reference books (like Bible dictionaries, commentaries, concordances), search online, listen to/watch sermons, and/or ask a mentor/parent/pastor. Record your findings below.

☐ 1. Whom was Jesus' sermon in Matthew 5, the Beatitudes, directed to?

☐ 2. What promises are found in Matthew 5 and to whom are they promised?

☐ 3. What blessings have you experienced in the midst of being insulted or persecuted because of your faith?

☐ My own question from yesterday

WANT TO KNOW MORE? CHECK OUT THIS BOOK!

Killing Christians: Living the Faith Where It's Not Safe to Believe, by Tom Doyle
witnesses.awanaym.org/library

ACTION PLAN

Based on what you have learned over the last five days about what it means to be a witness, create an action plan for yourself. What questions do you still need answered?

How would you encourage yourself in times of persecution and rejection?

NOTES

CITATION TRACK CHECKLIST >> 7.2

☐ DAYS 1-6
☐ CORE VERSES   LEADER'S INITIALS   DATE

ARE YOU ON TRACK WITH YOUR BIBLE READING? RECORD WHAT YOU READ HERE:

INTRO EXPERIENCE

Calculate the cost of your hobby.

$ _____

What is your hobby?

_____

How much time in the last seven days did you spend reading or learning about your hobby?

_____

How much time in the last seven days did you spend thinking about your hobby?

_____

How much time in the last seven days did you spend actively working on or doing your hobby?

_____

What was the cost of starting your hobby? (Ask your parents how much they may have spent too.)

$ _____

How much money have you or your parents spent in the last month on your hobby?

$ _____

What other opportunities have you given up in order to pursue or participate in your hobby?

_____

WATCH THE VIDEO
WITNESSES.AWANAYM.ORG

CORE CONTENT ××××××××××

Read Luke 9:57-62.

To be honest, Jesus seems completely unreasonable in today's reading from Luke 9. Three men seek to follow Jesus, but He seems to shut them all down. The first man tells Jesus he'll follow Him anywhere and Jesus tells him, *"Foxes have holes and birds of the air have nests, but the Son of Man has no place to lay His head"* (v. 58, NIV). In other words, following Christ is not easy and comfortable. Jesus calls a second man to follow Him and the man says he needs to bury his father first. But Jesus responds, *"Let the dead bury their own dead, but you go and proclaim the kingdom of God"* (v. 60, NIV). That's harsh! A third man tells Jesus he will follow Him but needs to say goodbye to his family first. Jesus replies, *"No one who puts his hand to the plow and looks back is fit for service in the kingdom of God"* (v. 62, NIV).

Couldn't Jesus wait for the man to say goodbye to his family? Burying the dead was a very important responsibility in Jesus' day. Why was Jesus so dismissive of it? And why did Jesus have to completely discourage the first man who sought to follow Him by letting him know how rough it would be? It's because Jesus wants true, dedicated followers who are going to place Him first, above all else. He let the last two men know that following Christ comes even before your own family.

Contrast this with the first time we see Jesus command someone to follow Him in Mark 1. Peter and his brother, Andrew, were fishing and Jesus told them to follow Him. What happened next? *At once they left their nets and followed Him* (v. 18, NIV). They made no excuses and did not tell Jesus to wait. They dropped their nets and followed Him immediately.

Jesus tells His disciples explicitly in Matthew 10:37-39: *"Anyone who loves his father or mother more than Me is not worthy of Me; anyone who loves his son or daughter more than Me is not worthy of Me; and anyone who does not take his cross and follow Me is not worthy of Me. Whoever finds his life will lose it, and whoever loses his life for My sake will find it"* (NIV). Like the three men from Luke 9, Jesus explained to His disciples that there is a cost to following Him. They needed to value Him even more than their own families and lives.

> **FOLLOW:** To act in accordance with someone's teaching and actions

There is a cost to being a witness for Christ. We may be rejected by family and friends. Missionaries leave the comfort and safety of familiar places and relationships to share the gospel. As we saw in our last lesson, we may even be persecuted for our faith and make the ultimate sacrifice for Christ. But remember that this was a sacrifice that God Himself was willing to make. The second person of the Trinity took on human flesh to live among us. He experienced weakness and hunger; He was rejected and ultimately killed.

Christ's sacrifice was more than we could ever imagine, bearing the sins of the world. For that, we owe Him everything. Jesus is trying to help those who desire to follow Him to know the costs. For you, it may not be leaving your family or giving up the comforts of your home, but committed followers are always asked to be willing to sacrifice in some way for the sake of the kingdom. Are you willing to count up the costs, invest, and sacrifice whatever it takes to be a true disciple?

BASED ON THE READING, WRITE A QUESTION YOU MIGHT HAVE.

CORE CONCEPT & VERSES

CORE CONCEPT:
Being a witness will at times require significant sacrifice.

READ & WRITE THESE VERSES: MATTHEW 16:24-25

Use the space below to help you remember these verses. Feel free to write, draw, or design in ways that make sense to you.

ABOUT THESE VERSES:

Chapter 16 of Matthew is usually recognized as Peter's confession of Jesus as Messiah, but we also see in this passage Jesus' first prediction of His crucifixion. And thus it serves as a teachable moment for the disciples regarding the cost of following Jesus. Immediately following Jesus' rebuke of Peter (v. 23), He turns to the rest of the disciples to remind them that suffering must be before glory, and humiliation before exaltation.

The imagery of the cross is horrifying to think about—especially for the first-century Roman world. The notion of picking up one's cross is likely derived from the requirement of a criminal to literally pick up the crossbeam and carry it to his execution. In one sense Jesus is speaking figuratively about one's spiritual life and the act of self-denial. However, in this context, Jesus is also speaking of the disciples giving their lives for the gospel.

▶ EXPLORATION QUESTIONS

Choose two questions from below. Spend the next two days exploring them. Feel free to use reference books (like Bible dictionaries, commentaries, concordances), search online, listen to/watch sermons, and/or ask a mentor/parent/pastor. Record your findings below.

☐ 1. What was wrong with the second man in Luke 9:59-60 wanting to bury his father first?

☐ 2. What lesson can be learned from the farmer and the plow in verses 61-62 about understanding the sacrifice it may cost us to follow Christ?

☐ 3. Besides His death, in what ways did Jesus sacrifice throughout His life and ministry?

☐ My own question from yesterday

WANT TO KNOW MORE? CHECK OUT THIS BOOK!

When Heaven and Earth Collide: Racism, Southern Evangelicals, and the Better Way of Jesus, by Alan Cross   witnesses.awanaym.org/library

▶ ACTION PLAN

Based on what you have learned over the last five days about what it means to be a witness, create an action plan for yourself. What questions do you still need answered?

What have you put before God?

▶ NOTES

CITATION TRACK CHECKLIST >> 7.3

- DAYS 1-6
- CORE VERSES   LEADER'S INITIALS   DATE

ARE YOU ON TRACK WITH YOUR BIBLE READING? RECORD WHAT YOU READ HERE:

love

▶ INTRO EXPERIENCE

In the midst of division and chaos in this world, there are still endless stories of love extending beyond human dividing lines. Find a story of someone demonstrating love across man-made boundaries. Copy the story in your book. If you see it, include the motivation of the loving act. Also, include a photo from the story or create an image to help solidify the story of love in your memory.

▶ **WATCH THE VIDEO**
WITNESSES.AWANAYM.ORG

CORE CONTENT ✕ ✕ ✕ ✕ ✕ ✕ ✕ ✕ ✕ ✕ ✕

Read Luke 6:27-36.

Love. It's the greatest thing in the world. Countless songs, poems, and movies have been created to celebrate love. There's nothing better than loving someone else and being loved in return. And love is what the entire Christian life is all about. After all, … *God is love (1 John 4:8)*.

1 Corinthians 13, the great chapter of love, tells us that even if we give all we have to the poor or gain all the knowledge in the world, if we don't have love, it's all meaningless. When the Pharisees asked Jesus what the greatest commandment was, He replied it was to love God with all that we are, and the second is to love your neighbor (Matthew 22:38-40). Paul echoes this in Galatians, stating that the entire Law could be summarized as to love your neighbor (Galatians 5:14).

John is called the apostle of love because he wrote of love so much in his Gospel and letters. He penned the famous John 3:16, which tells us that God sent us His Son to save us because of His great love for us. Also in John's Gospel, Jesus told His disciples that others would know they were His followers by their love for each other (13:35). He also said that there is no greater love than to lay down your life for your friends (15:13).

But in today's reading from Luke 6, we are instructed to love more than just our friends, family, and fellow Christians, the ones who love us back. Jesus commanded: "… *Love your enemies, do good to those who hate you, bless those who curse you, pray for those who mistreat you*" (v. 27, NIV). It's difficult enough to love our parents when they don't always let us have our way, or to love our annoying younger siblings. Jesus wants us to love people who hate us and who mistreat us. That means loving the bully at school, or another who has mistreated you.

> **MERCY:** An act of compassion toward an offender or enemy

This is what shows the world that we are different, that we mean business. We love everyone. We aren't nice to people just to gain their favor or to manipulate them. We love them just because they are valuable, being bearers of God's image.

Verse 29 begins, *If someone strikes you on one cheek, turn to him the other also.* Love bears insults and does not retaliate. The second half of the verse says, *If someone takes your cloak, do not stop him from taking your tunic* (NIV). Even when people steal from us, when they purposely take advantage of us, we are still to love them and be generous to them.

Verse 35 says that God *is kind to the ungrateful and wicked* (NIV). And that is what we were before God saved us. While we were still in our sin, we were enemies with God (see Romans 5). But God died for us because He loved us so much. So if God could love us while we were His enemies, shouldn't we love our enemies too?

This is how we are the greatest witnesses, not by loving people who are lovable, but by loving people the world sees as unlovable, giving to those who cannot give back, taking insults, and not fighting back. This is what it means to be true witnesses. This is what will show the world that Jesus lives within us.

BASED ON THE READING, WRITE A QUESTION YOU MIGHT HAVE.

CORE CONCEPT & VERSES

CORE CONCEPT:
We cannot properly communicate the gospel without first loving others.

READ & WRITE THESE VERSES: LUKE 6:27-28

*Use the space below to help you remember these verses.
Feel free to write, draw, or design in ways that make sense to you.*

ABOUT THESE VERSES

Although much shorter, Luke's version of the Sermon on the Mount holds similar importance to Matthew's account. Compared to over 100 verses in Matthew, Luke's account of Jesus' teaching is only 30 verses. He remains focused on the major themes and principles of Jesus' words and omits much of the Jewish legalism because it did not pertain to his primary audience, the Gentiles.

It is in this week's verses that we find the central point of the sermon—what it means to be a disciple of Jesus. Luke wants to make sure his readers understand that the actions of a true disciple will reflect true love and true righteousness that stem from the Spirit of God. Jesus describes this kind of love using the imagery of being disrespected or disgraced—taking the act of love well beyond the accepted social norms.

EXPLORATION QUESTIONS

Choose two questions from below. Spend the next two days exploring them. Feel free to use reference books (like Bible dictionaries, commentaries, concordances), search online, listen to/watch sermons, and/or ask a mentor/parent/pastor. Record your findings below.

☐ 1. What did slapping on the cheek symbolize in Jesus' day and what would be the equivalent today (v. 29)?

☐ 2. Which Greek word for love was used in this passage and what is the meaning of that particular word for love?

☐ 3. Luke gives us several reasons for loving our enemies. List and explain as many as you can find in this passage.

☐ My own question from yesterday

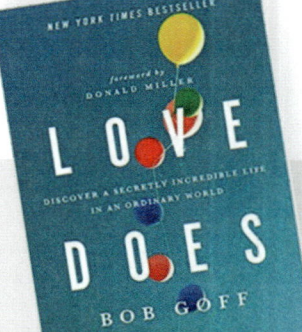

WANT TO KNOW MORE? CHECK OUT THIS BOOK!

Love Does: Discover a Secretly Incredible Life in an Ordinary World, by Bob Goff
witnesses.awanaym.org/library

ACTION PLAN

Based on what you have learned over the last five days about what it means to be a witness, create an action plan for yourself. What questions do you still need answered?

What is your plan when someone mistreats you? Write two or three responses you will use

Learn how kids in the persecuted church respond to hatred with love.
VISIT AWANA.ORG/GOGLOBAL

NOTES

CITATION TRACK CHECKLIST >> 7.4

DAYS 1-6

CORE VERSES   LEADER'S INITIALS   DATE

ARE YOU ON TRACK WITH YOUR BIBLE READING? RECORD WHAT YOU READ HERE:

 **WATCH THE VIDEO**
awanaym.org/videos

LEAD
UNIT 08

Hey friends,

The time has come to return home. And we've covered a lot of ground! We've asked many questions and found answers that have carried both fire and light to guide our feet in the dark. All there's left to ask ourselves is how do we put it all together? How do we grab everything we've learned and move forward with it? At least that's what's on my mind.

Let's remember this. Graciously and confidently sharing our faith with others makes awakening possible. Not because of our skills, charisma, or eloquence, but because of God's overwhelming conviction and grace stirring up the dirt in their hearts. And our willingness to share Jesus will inspire others to do the same. So let your focus be to do nothing more than to speak the love and truth of Jesus.

Mentors have made a powerful, long-term impact on my faith journey. So I highly encourage you to seek mature Christians to be your mentors. But also, seek opportunities to mentor others and pass down what you have learned and witnessed for yourself. With that, you'll learn to lead. Because as Jesus leads us, He calls us to lead others, following His example. Hand in hand, we move forward together. The most beautiful thing about my network of mentors is that we witness, encourage, teach, and practice vulnerability with each other. There are stories to be heard, with plenty of wisdom and prayer needs to be shared.

To show you just what I mean, I sat down with my mentors and unpacked pieces of this journey with them. Then I headed back to my literal home base, home sweet home, and got my pencils ready. I noted my favorite sayings and reminders from throughout the journey, and created a new routine for myself moving forward. And I challenge you to also sit down and jot down your biggest takeaways in this journey. So flip through your book, find old notes, and decode those scribbles! Then write a list somewhere you'll see often to remember them. Check in with friends to refresh your memory, and to hear what takeaways shook them.

This is spiritual food to nourish real faith. And I want to thank you for bravely walking this out with me. And God, who is so good and so kind, to give me the opportunity to do what I love in ways I never imagined. But it's true what they say. A crooked stick can still draw a straight line. If God can transform and use someone like me, I certainly believe that He hopes to do the same for someone like you.

Your co-adventurer,

Kelly Carolini

awakening

▶ INTRO EXPERIENCE

Throughout history, music has had an incredible impact on culture, politics, and, some would even argue the world. Songs have a way of spreading a message that hooks people and inspires them to move and act. Research a song that has changed the world and complete the following.

Name of song:

Artist:

Year released:

Brief description of the culture at the time:

Summary of the song's message:

What risk did the artist take in releasing this song?

How did the song impact the world?

▶ WATCH THE VIDEO
WITNESSES.AWANAYM.ORG

CORE CONTENT ×××××××××××

Read Acts 4:32-35.

The Great Awakening was a time of revival in American and European history in the mid-18th century. Christians were "awakened" from passivity and called to a more robust spiritual life, spurred by powerful sermons from preachers such as Jonathan Edwards and George Whitefield. There have been other awakening periods throughout American history and many great preachers, such as Billy Graham, known for their revival services. In today's world we have the incredible opportunity to experience another great awakening.

> **AWAKENING:** When a revival of the church spreads to the wider society

In this reading we see the early church awakened to a brand-new reality where it can experience the power of the Holy Spirit, which was a new thing, and the present kingdom of God. It was so beautiful and appealing that others were inspired and moved to join them.

First, everyone was *one in heart and mind* (v. 32, NIV). Unity is essential to revival. Prior to His crucifixion, Jesus prayed to the Father that His followers would be one as He and the Father were one, that they would be in complete unity (John 17:20-23). As we learned in our last lesson, our love for each other is a sign that we are true followers of Christ. All throughout the New Testament, believers are called to unity in mind and spirit.

Second, the believers had a community-minded generosity. Early Christians shared everything. They based their lives and livelihood on a mindset that no one would go without. The community pooled its resources. They gave whatever and everything they had so there was no one left in need (v. 34). They even sold off their houses and land and gave the money from the sales. Christians are called to participate in their community and give generously.

Third, the believers preached the gospel. Verse 33 says: *With great power the apostles continued to testify to the resurrection of the Lord Jesus ...* (NIV). The resurrection of Jesus Christ was a history-altering event. As we saw in the lesson on fear, it changed the disciples from a collection of cowards to bold witnesses, willing to suffer and lay down their lives for the truth. When you've encountered the life-changing power of the gospel, you can't keep it to yourself, no matter what the cost. The resurrection promises a new life to all who believe. What could be greater news than that?

> **REVIVAL:** A community of faith returning to their devotion to God

The three components to revival are simple: unity, generosity, and preaching the gospel. We catch a glimpse of this every Sunday in our worship services. But we need to turn up the passion. Show greater love to your brothers and sisters in Christ. Encourage each other. Be generous. And preach the gospel. Be bold. Be a witness in word and set an example for everyone around you.

The faithfulness of Peter and John inspired the early church to move, trust Jesus, and make disciples. The people caught a glimpse of the Holy Spirit working through the first disciples and they wanted to be a part of it. Our willingness to be bold witnesses for Christ just might set someone else's passion afire to do the same. Don't wait for the next famous preacher or megachurch; the spirit of God is waiting to work through you!

BASED ON THE READING, WRITE A QUESTION YOU MIGHT HAVE.

CORE CONCEPT & VERSE

CORE CONCEPT:
My willingness to share Christ will inspire others to do the same.

READ & WRITE THIS VERSE: ACTS 4:33

*Use the space below to help you remember this verse.
Feel free to write, draw, or design in ways that make sense to you.*

ABOUT THIS VERSE:

The early chapters of Acts provide us with a detailed account of the rise of the early church and we get a glimpse of how the Holy Spirit is living and active among the disciples. But we also see how the Roman world responded. From Peter's message in Chapter 2 to the healing of the lame man in Chapter 3, we find in Chapter 4 that the Jewish religious leadership responds by attempting to silence Peter and John.

It was the insistence of Peter and John to follow the command of Christ rather than the command of the Pharisees and teachers of the Law that compelled and motivated the rest of the Church. Rather than hiding out and protecting themselves, Peter, John, and the rest of the Church became even bolder and empowered by the Spirit to carry the gospel forward.

▶ EXPLORATION QUESTIONS

Choose two questions from below. Spend the next two days exploring them. Feel free to use reference books (like Bible dictionaries, commentaries, concordances), search online, listen to/watch sermons, and/or ask a mentor/parent/pastor. Record your findings below.

☐ 1. What three components of spiritual revival do we see in this passage?

☐ 2. Do you see any spiritual revival or awakening happening today, and if so, what are the indicators of it?

☐ 3. What verse, from this passage or not, is inspiring you most to speak the gospel and why?

☐ My own question from yesterday

WANT TO KNOW MORE? CHECK OUT THIS BOOK!

Get Real: Sharing Your Everyday Faith Every Day, by John S. Leonard
witnesses.awanaym.org/library

▶ ACTION PLAN

Based on what you have learned over the last five days about what it means to be a witness, create an action plan for yourself. What questions do you still need answered?

Write a prayer about your current attitude toward witnessing.

▶ NOTES

CITATION TRACK CHECKLIST >> 8.1

☐ DAYS 1-6
☐ CORE VERSES   LEADER'S INITIALS _____   DATE _____

ARE YOU ON TRACK WITH YOUR BIBLE READING? RECORD WHAT YOU READ HERE:

▶ INTRO EXPERIENCE

Track your thoughts and actions. This week keep a running journal of things you think about and another on how you've acted. Much of it will be likely be about school and responsibilities you need to fulfill, but how do you occupy your mind and motivations in between those duties? This is a private activity. You won't be asked to share specifics with the group, but it's good accountability for you to get a summary of what occupies your brainpower.

Sunday:

Monday:

Tuesday:

Wednesday:

Thursday:

Friday:

Saturday:

After your week of keeping track, answer these questions.
Were you surprised by anything?

Were you disappointed by anything?

▶ WATCH THE VIDEO
WITNESSES.AWANAYM.ORG

CORE CONTENT

Read Acts 4:1-31.

We've all met obsessive people, people who won't stop talking about their favorite sports teams, politics, music, television, movies, that amazing person they just met and are totally going to spend the rest of their lives with. Most things people obsess over are trivial and meaningless in the grand scheme of life. But what does it mean to be obsessed with the gospel? That's what we see in today's reading.

> **OBSESSION:** A persistent and consuming thought or idea

In Acts 3, God works through Peter to heal a man who was lame from birth. He and John use this opportunity to preach the resurrection of Jesus, and the religious leaders don't like it. Acts 4 begins with Peter and John being arrested. The religious leaders ask them under what authority they can perform miracles and Peter, filled with the Spirit, takes the opportunity to again preach Jesus' resurrection and that salvation is through Christ alone. The religious leaders were amazed because Peter and John were average, unschooled men (v. 13). They didn't know what to do since it was such a public miracle, so they let Peter and John go with a warning to stop preaching in Jesus' name.

But did they listen? Of course not! Peter and John reply that it is more important to listen to God than to men. And here we see our key verse: *For we cannot help speaking about what we have seen and heard* (v. 20, NIV).

These men were truly obsessed with Christ. They had been thrown in prison (and it wouldn't be the last time). As we have seen in previous lessons, following Christ requires sacrifice and can even lead to persecution. But there is nothing more important in this world than to be a witness for Christ. And Peter and John continued to model this in Acts 4.

When they were released, they went back to their people and, instead of fearing imprisonment again, they were emboldened. They praised God and even prayed for more boldness in the face of their struggles and to perform even more signs and wonders in Jesus' name. Once their prayer was over, verse 31 tells us *the place where they were meeting was shaken. And they were all filled with the Holy Spirit and spoke the word of God boldly* (NIV). Wow!

That is the power of the gospel. As witnesses for Christ, we have the truth and so we need to share it with others. And think about how this all started with just two men, Peter and John. Their obsession for spreading the gospel became contagious and affected the entire believing community. Like the last lesson said, revival can begin with you!

Do you truly believe that *Salvation is found in no one else, for there is no other name under heaven given to men by which we must be saved* (v. 12, NIV), that the world is hopelessly, spiritually lost without Jesus? Once you understand the importance of the gospel, you will be like Peter and John who, even after being warned to be silent, said, *... We cannot help speaking about what we have seen and heard* (v. 20, NIV). Forget all of the trivial things that people obsess over in this life and commit yourself to being a witness for Christ with all that you are.

BASED ON THE READING, WRITE A QUESTION YOU MIGHT HAVE.

CORE CONCEPT & VERSE

CORE CONCEPT:
I can do nothing but speak of the love of Jesus.

READ & WRITE THIS VERSE: ACTS 4:20

Use the space below to help you remember this verse. Feel free to write, draw, or design in ways that make sense to you.

ABOUT THE VERSE

Throughout Acts, Luke describes several firsts of the Church: the first message of the good news, the first healing, and in the case of Chapter 4, the first persecution. It is this first persecution of Peter and John by Jewish authorities for relentlessly sharing the gospel message that sets the stage for later and more intense persecution—ultimately leading to the death of Stephen in Chapter 7, the persecution under Saul before he is converted in Chapter 9.

This week's verse gives us some key insight into how the gospel and the power of the Spirit impacted the first disciples. Refusing to recognize what Peter and John had witnessed, the resurrection of Christ, would be impossible. It is in this verse that we encounter the essence of what it means to be a witness.

▶ EXPLORATION QUESTIONS

Choose two questions from below. Spend the next two days exploring them. Feel free to use reference books (like Bible dictionaries, commentaries, concordances), search online, listen to/watch sermons, and/or ask a mentor/parent/pastor. Record your findings below.

☐ 1. What did the disciples risk to share the gospel with others?

☐ 2. Why were the disciples so committed and compelled to share the gospel?

☐ 3. Whom do you know that is obsessed with sharing the gospel? Explain.

☐ My own question from yesterday

WANT TO KNOW MORE? CHECK OUT THIS BOOK!

Radical, by David Platt
witnesses.awanaym.org/library

▶ ACTION PLAN

Based on what you have learned over the last five days about what it means to be a witness, create an action plan for yourself. What questions do you still need answered?

How will you fulfill God's command to make disciples?

▶ NOTES

CITATION TRACK CHECKLIST >> 8.2

- DAYS 1-6
- CORE VERSES   LEADER'S INITIALS   DATE

ARE YOU ON TRACK WITH YOUR BIBLE READING? RECORD WHAT YOU READ HERE

▶ INTRO EXPERIENCE

Make a list of people you could seek out for spiritual advice. List at least three.

Name:	Why did you choose this person?

▶ WATCH THE VIDEO
WITNESSES.AWANAYM.ORG

CORE CONTENT

Read 1 Thessalonians 1.

Elijah mentored Elisha. Paul mentored Timothy. Jesus mentored His disciples. Likewise, many other Christians probably mentored you in your life: your parents, your pastor, your Sunday school teachers. Mentoring is an important part of the Christian walk. We see this in today's reading from Paul's first letter to the Thessalonians.

Paul was the original church planter. Not only did he go around preaching the gospel, but he also established communities of believers. And he also did not merely start churches and move on. He would visit them and write letters to check on them from time to time, praising them for the good and chastising them for the bad. Here we have an example of the good.

We see in 1 Thessalonians 1:2-3 that this church was very dear to Paul, as he continually prayed for them, remembering their love and good works. This is all because Paul took the time to live with them and be an example for the church, which they then imitated (vv. 5-6). Because of this, they *became a model to all the believers in Macedonia and Achaia* and so their *faith in God has become known everywhere* (vv. 7-8, NIV). That's quite the witness!

The Thessalonian church had a tremendous influence on the world around them. But it all began with Paul, Timothy, and Silas. Because they took the time and effort to pour into the church community, the Thessalonians then followed their example and impacted their surrounding communities. This is exactly how the gospel is supposed to spread, by Christians being mentored by someone and then turning around and being an example for others.

It's important to share the gospel with everyone we can. But that's only part of our responsibility. Once someone has placed his faith in Christ, he's going to need to learn what it means to be a Christian. And merely handing him a Bible and saying, "Read it" isn't enough. He'll need someone to help guide him, to assist in navigating the difficult parts of the Bible, to keep him accountable. And once he has grown enough spiritually, it is his job to then find someone for him to mentor.

Jesus' last command to His followers prior to his ascension was ... *Go and make disciples of all nations ... (Matthew 28:19*, NIV). There are two things to note from this. First, Jesus did not just tell His followers to go around evangelizing. He wanted them to make disciples of their own. Jesus lived with them and taught them, they should do the same with others. Also, Jesus wanted His message to go to all nations. This was obviously not something those He was directly addressing would be able to do all by themselves. They would need to enlist others to continue the mission, so that the gospel could spread to the entire world. Jesus formed His own disciples, and then they were to go and do the same.

> **SPIRITUAL MENTOR:**
> An experienced and trusted Christian who gives advice and guidance

Think about those who mentored you in your Christian life. Now think about your friends or your younger family members. How can you be a mentor for them? As a witness, God wants you to mentor someone else, to continue the mission of the original disciples *and make disciples of all nations.*

BASED ON THE READING, WRITE A QUESTION YOU MIGHT HAVE.

CORE CONCEPT & VERSES

CORE CONCEPT:
We must seek mature Christians to be mentors, but must also endeavor to mentor others.

READ & WRITE THESE VERSES: LUKE 6:39-40

Use the space below to help you remember these verses. Feel free to write, draw, or design in ways that make sense to you.

ABOUT THESE VERSES:

Up to this point in Chapter 6 of Luke, Jesus has addressed the conduct of disciples and the choices they ought to make. In the last part of the chapter, Jesus shifts His tone slightly. He moves from simply giving one command after another to parables that are descriptive of what it looks like to be a disciple able to disciple another. These two examples Jesus gives help paint a picture of the important relationship between student and teacher.

The first example speaks to the responsibility of the student. They are to learn so that they can teach others. The second example is the responsibility of the teacher to stay sharp and educated. The command here is simple, but important: Be careful whom you follow and how people follow you.

▶ EXPLORATION QUESTIONS

Choose two questions from below. Spend the next two days exploring them. Feel free to use reference books (like Bible dictionaries, commentaries, concordances), search online, listen to/watch sermons, and/or ask a mentor/parent/pastor. Record your findings below.

☐ 1. What were Timothy's and Silas' relationships to Paul?

☐ 2. Look up 1 Thessalonians 1:6, Philippians 3:17, and 1 Corinthians 11:1. What do they all have in common?

☐ 3. In verse 7 Paul gives a reason to follow his example. What was his reason and the purpose of having a mentor?

☐ My own question from yesterday

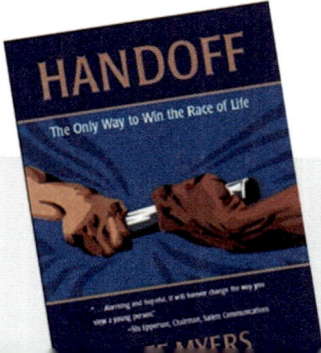

WANT TO KNOW MORE? CHECK OUT THIS BOOK!

Handoff: The Only Way to Win the Race of Life, by Jeff Myers
witnesses.awanaym.org/library

ACTION PLAN

Based on what you have learned over the last five days about what it means to be a witness, create an action plan for yourself. What questions do you still need answered? If you don't already have a mentor, ask your parents, small group leader, or pastor for a suggestion.

MY PLAN

NOTES

CITATION TRACK CHECKLIST >> 8.3

- DAYS 1-6
- CORE VERSES   LEADER'S INITIALS   DATE

ARE YOU ON TRACK WITH YOUR BIBLE READING? RECORD WHAT YOU READ HERE:

INTRO EXPERIENCE

List at least four people who are important to you.	List at least four things you value the most. These could be possessions or personal characteristics.	List four experiences, good or bad, that have shaped you as a person (i.e., learning experiences).

List four specific goals that are important to you in your future life.	List four places that are important to you or that God has brought to your attention.	List your interests, skills, and/or talents.

WATCH THE VIDEO
WITNESSES.AWANAYM.ORG

CORE CONTENT ✕ ✕ ✕ ✕ ✕ ✕ ✕ ✕ ✕ ✕ ✕

Read Joshua 1.

Today's reading tells of the change in leadership for God's people. Moses had the great task of leading the Israelites out of Egypt, but his time on earth had ended. It was time for a new leader to replace him: Joshua. Moses had begun the journey to the Promised Land and it was up to Joshua to complete it. While God is speaking directly to Joshua in the reading, it contains principles that are important for any Christian leader.

In verse 5, God tells Joshua, ... *I will never leave you nor forsake you* (NIV). And that's why He can tell Joshua in the very next verse to *be strong and courageous*. In fact, God says this two more times, in verses 7 and 9. Again, He reiterates that *the LORD your God will be with you wherever you go* (v. 9, NIV). As we discussed in our lesson on fear, it is natural to be afraid. That's why God tells Joshua three times in a span of four verses to *be strong and courageous*! We must constantly remind ourselves that God is always with us and we can find our safety and comfort in Him. Like the psalmist said: *Where can I go from Your Spirit? Where can I flee from Your presence? If I go up to the heavens, You are there; if I make my bed in the depths, You are there (Psalm 139:7-8,* NIV). No matter where we go and regardless of how hard things get, God is there with us. So as you go about as a witness, *be strong and courageous*, for God is always with you.

God also gives a crucial command to ... *Be careful to obey all the law My servant Moses gave you; do not turn from it to the right or to the left* and ... *Do not let this Book of the Law depart from your mouth; meditate on it day and night, so that you may be careful to do everything written in it ..."* (vv. 7-8, NIV). We are to do the same! We must always be immersed in God's Word. It is our source of spiritual life. We need constant reminders of what God has done for us and what He will continue to do.

After Joshua has given his orders to the people, they then commit themselves to Joshua's leadership. They promise to follow his commands and obey him as they obeyed Moses before him (vv. 16-17). Then they tell Joshua to *be strong and courageous*, just as God told him (v. 18). Being a leader is a huge responsibility, one that cannot be taken lightly. But the people you lead will also be your strength.

> **LEAD:** To inspire or motivate someone to move or change from one thing or place to another

As we end our study, remember once again what God told Joshua, ... *I will never leave you nor forsake you* (v. 5). He will never leave nor forsake you either. Be strong and courageous. You can face fear and persecution because God is always with you. Use everything you have learned this year to be a witness for Christ, both in word and by example. Like Paul, be someone who says, *Follow my example, as I follow the example of Christ (1 Corinthians 11:1,* NIV).

BASED ON THE READING, WRITE A QUESTION YOU MIGHT HAVE.

_____

_____

_____

_____

CORE CONCEPT & VERSE

CORE CONCEPT:
As we are led by Christ, we are called to lead others to Him.

READ & WRITE THIS VERSE: PSALM 71:18

Use the space below to help you remember this verse.
Feel free to write, draw, or design in ways that make sense to you.

ABOUT THE VERSE

This psalm, by an unnamed writer, is a cry for help. It is a cry for help, yet resounding in confidence in God. The psalmist has trusted God for many years and begins his poem expressing that confidence. We are not certain what kind of attack he was under, but he required deliverance and was insistent on waiting for the hand of God to intervene.

The writer details the mighty acts of God. It is the promises and faithfulness of God that not only provide him the strength to wait, but a message to pass down from generation to generation. This psalm not only declares God's great power to deliver and a man's cry for that help, but an incredible testimony of a man who wants God's renown to be known to generations to come.

EXPLORATION QUESTIONS

Choose two questions from below. Spend the next two days exploring them. Feel free to use reference books (like Bible dictionaries, commentaries, concordances), search online, listen to/watch sermons, and/or ask a mentor/parent/pastor. Record your findings below.

☐ 1. The name Yeshua (Joshua) is the Hebrew version of the Greek name Jesus. Who was Joshua and what other similarities did he have with Jesus?

☐ 2. Verses 6-9 lay out requirements and promises for Joshua as he leads. What are the conditions and rewards promised in these verses?

☐ 3. What challenges and encouragement do you take away from this passage?

☐ My own question from yesterday

WANT TO KNOW MORE? CHECK OUT THIS BOOK!

How to Lead When You're Not in Charge: Leveraging Influence When You Lack Authority, by Clay Scroggins   witnesses.awanaym.org/library

ACTION PLAN

Based on what you have learned over the last five days about what it means to be a witness, create an action plan for yourself. What questions do you still need answered? Whom are you currently leading toward Christ?

NOTES

CITATION TRACK CHECKLIST >> 8.4

☐ DAYS 1-6
☐ CORE VERSES   LEADER'S INITIALS   DATE

ARE YOU ON TRACK WITH YOUR BIBLE READING? RECORD WHAT YOU READ HERE:

OLD TESTAMENT READING PLAN

In order for a leader to initial, you need to have read the book of the Bible, completed the summary, and recited the verse. Learn more about Bible Summaries at awanaym.org/bible-reading-summaries.

LEADER'S INITIALS

- **LEVITICUS 20:7-8**

- **RUTH 1:16**

- **ISAIAH 53:11**

- **DANIEL 2:21**

- **HOSEA 2:19**

- **AMOS 5:24**

- **NAHUM 1:7**

- **HABAKKUK 2:4**

- **MALACHI 3:7**

LEADER'S INITIALS   DATE

SHARE YOUR FAITH

In order for your leader to sign off on this section, you need to have at least one spiritually significant conversation with a nonbeliever about your faith and the gospel. Describe the experience and your conversation in the space below.

LEADER'S INITIALS   DATE

MAJOR AWARDS

Throughout Scripture, awards are given in recognition of special achievement or obedience. Awana values the commitment students demonstrate for growing in their faith. These are the major awards a student may receive in Trek® and Journey:

TIMOTHY AWARD = 4 YEARS OF WORK COMPLETED

MERITORIOUS AWARD = 6 YEARS OF WORK COMPLETED

CITATION AWARD = 10 YEARS OF WORK COMPLETED

IN JOURNEY, A YEAR OF WORK INCLUDES COMPLETING ...

- Faith Foundation
  (Entrance booklet to be completed once when student starts the Journey program)
- Bible Study
- Bible summaries
- Share your faith.
- Attend a Christian training seminar.
- Participate in long-term service project.

See Awanaym.org/awards to learn more about each requirement and to download the free Citation matrix for easy achievement tracking.

SCHOLARSHIPS

Our college and university network connects students with opportunities for ongoing education by rewarding them with financial scholarships from quality institutions. Recognizing the high caliber of students that emerge from Awana Youth Ministries™, these schools are eager to provide scholarships for students who have reached various levels of achievement within the Awana curriculum.

For a list of current scholarships available from our college and university network, please visit *awanaym.org/scholarships*.